The Heart of Centering Prayer

Centering Prayer and Inner Awakening

Chanting the Psalms

The Holy Trinity and the Law of Three:
Discovering the Radical Truth at the Heart of Christianity

Love Is Stronger Than Death:
The Mystical Union of Two Souls

The Meaning of Mary Magdalene:
Discovering the Woman at the Heart of Christianity

Mystical Hope: Trusting in the Mercy of God

The Wisdom Jesus:
Transforming Heart and Mind—
A New Perspective on Christ and His Message

The Wisdom Way of Knowing:
Reclaiming an Ancient Tradition to Awaken the Heart

The Heart of Centering Prayer

Nondual Christianity in Theory and Practice

Cynthia Bourgeault

SHAMBHALA
Boulder
2016

Shambhala Publications, Inc.
4720 Walnut Street
Boulder, Colorado 80301
www.shambhala.com

9 8 7 6 5 4 3 2

Printed in the United States of America

⊛ This edition is printed on acid-free paper that meets the American National Standards Institute z39.48 Standard.

♻ This book is printed on 30% post-consumer recycled paper. For more information please visit www.shambhala.com.

Distributed in the United States by Penguin Random House LLC and in Canada by Random House of Canada Ltd

Designed by Greta D. Sibley

Library of Congress Cataloging-in-Publication Data
Names: Bourgeault, Cynthia, author.
Title: The heart of centering prayer: nondual Christianity in theory and practice / Cynthia Bourgeault.
Description: First Edition. | Boulder: Shambhala, 2016. | Includes bibliographical references and index.
Identifiers: LCCN 2016013201 | ISBN 9781611803143 (pbk.: alk. paper)
Subjects: LCSH: Contemplation. | Spiritual life—Christianity.
Classification: LCC BV5091.C7 B685 2016 | DDC 248.3—dc23
LC record available at https://lccn.loc.gov/2016013201

to Thomas Keating

Beloved teacher,
spiritual father,
and friend

CONTENTS

ACKNOWLEDGMENTS

I am deeply grateful to the Narthex Foundation for the financial support that allowed me to carve time out of my teaching schedule to bring this book together.

Some of the material here has been previously published or offered in other teaching formats. While it has all been reworked extensively to fit its new habitat, I acknowledge herewith, with gratitude, my original publishing partners. What is now part one, "A Short Course on Centering Prayer," originated as a twelve-week e-course offered by Spirituality and Practice in the fall of 2011. My continuing thanks to Fred and Mary Ann Brussat for their imaginative programming and brilliant website: you guys are truly pioneers! My present chapter 3, "Centering Prayer and Attention of the Heart," originally appeared as an essay (by that same title but with a somewhat different focus) in *The Merton Annual,* vol. 20 (2007). My present chapter 4, "Centering Prayer as Witnessing Practice," was originally published (again by the same title) in the *Sewanee Theological Review,* vol. 53, no. 3 (Pentecost 2010). My extensive exploration of *The Cloud of Unknowing,* which comprises part three of this present book, began as a keynote address to Contemplative Outreach of Colorado in March 2013; it was further developed as part of a teaching unit for The Living School for Action and Contemplation, where I have the honor of serving as one of the core faculty. To my colleagues Richard Rohr and Jim Finley, to the curriculum director Paul Swanson, and to all those pilot Living School students who first worked their way through this material, thank you for your adventurous spirits and helpful feedback.

I am particularly grateful to Michael Spezio and Brent Field, who took the time to walk me through their groundbreaking neuroscience research on Centering Prayer and to review my chapter 6 for accuracy.

To Dave O'Neal, my veteran editorial partner at Shambhala (I think this makes book number five, yes?), for your inimitable way of holding my feet to the fire while still drawing out, with such respect and finesse, so much more than I knew was in me.

And to Thomas Keating, teacher, friend, guide, angel-to-my-Jacob, and nest for my soul for thirty-five years, there are no words that can even begin to express what you have meant in my life. Just know that the simple "thank you" conveyed in this dedication reverberates with a love that is bigger than both of us and will continue to hold us together. Of this I am sure.

The Heart *of* Centering Prayer

Introduction

It's been more than a decade now since I wrote *Centering Prayer and Inner Awakening.*[1] During these years, Centering Prayer has continued to be the mainstay of my spiritual practice, and my thinking on it has continued to evolve. The book you're now holding in your hands is really the paper trail of that evolution. In format, it draws together some of my major talks and writings on Centering Prayer over these past ten years. But don't take that to mean that this is simply an anthology, a new collection of already published articles. Beneath the surface of all those presentations, a unifying thread has slowly been taking shape, and the purpose of this book is to draw it out and look at some of its implications, both for Centering Prayer itself and for the greater Christian contemplative tradition in which it is ensconced. Some of you may have encountered portions of this material before; I doubt that any of you have encountered *all* of it or put the pieces together in the way that I am about to do here.

While these talks and essays were originally developed in a variety of formats and presentational styles, they all step off from the common underlying assumption *that Centering Prayer is a distinctive method of meditation with its own way of getting there.* While this assertion may seem obvious to those of you actually practicing the prayer, I find that it continues to be significantly underappreciated by those merely commenting on it, whether from a scientific, theological, or interspiritual perspective. Again and again, in the spate of new materials emerging from all these quarters, I encounter the assumption that there is what you might call a "standard model" of meditation, and that Centering Prayer simply happens to be the Christian packaging of it. The radical import of Thomas Keating's oft quoted dictum that "Centering Prayer is done not with attention but with *intention*" generally fails to register.

So my first task in this book will be to bring some consideration to the method of Centering Prayer—not so much from the "why" of the method as from the "how" of it, or what actually happens when you're doing the practice. And here, in contrast to what most people assume to be the "standard model" of meditation, Centering Prayer does indeed seem to be playing by a whole different set of rules. Rather than engaging the powers of focused attention (on the breath, a mantra), it seems to be more interested in cultivating two qualities that essentially involve the *release* of attention (or perhaps, more accurately, its reconfiguration). The first of these qualities has been extensively described in the Orthodox branch of Christianity under the name of "attention of the heart" (although of course without any awareness of its relevance for Centering Prayer). The second, to the best of my knowledge, has never been specifically identified in the Christian tradition at all, although it has been accurately and even comprehensively described, as we will see in part three of this book. A Tibetan Buddhist would have no difficulty spotting it as *objectless awareness*.

Both of these capacities are well known within any comprehensive taxonomy of meditation. But in the Eastern traditions, they are generally assumed to be *advanced* capacities, accessed only after a conscious voluntary attention has been well established. What makes Centering Prayer so charmingly disconcerting is that it *leads off* with these capacities, essentially turning traditional meditation pedagogy on its head. This was largely the innovation of Father Thomas Keating, principal architect of Centering Prayer and my own mentor in the practice for more than thirty years now. Whether his intuition on this point proves in the long run to be a stroke of genius or an ill-advised shortcut is for me one of the more interesting questions still out there to be addressed. As my presentation unfolds, I think you will come to see how I feel about this and why.

Since I have introduced the word "nondual" into my title (with the implicit claim that Centering Prayer has some contributions to make in this regard), I realize I should probably at this point clarify what I mean by this term. While the word is obviously trendy in contemporary spiritual literature, it's been obvious to me as I make my teaching rounds that most Christians are largely clueless about what's actually involved here and use the term in a variety of confused and contradictory ways.

The confusion may be attributable in large part to the fact that "nondual" is a relative newcomer to the Western spiritual lexicon, having gained widespread currency only in the latter half of the century along with the emergence of interspiritual dialogue and those popular contemporary maps of the levels of consciousness as articulated by Ken Wilber, Spiral Dynamics, and others. In the more familiar Christian road map, which guided spiritual progress in both Christian East and Christian West for more than a millennium, the traditional way of designating that upper echelon of spiritual attainment would have been "unitive" (as in "purgative," "illuminative," and "unitive" ways). But it is a fundamental miscalculation to assume that these terms equate directly, since the measuring rods used to determine them are so very different. The road map in Christianity is not based on levels of consciousness but on progressive degrees of union whose descriptions are for the most part affective rather than cognitive. This results in a kind of continuous "apples and oranges" situation, in which the rhapsodic "mystical marriage" metaphors dominating so much of the Christian discussion of unitive experience are misinterpreted as evidence of an immature level of consciousness (still characterized by personal desire) rather than as an oblique way of pointing toward a kind of transformation that does not ultimately occur on the cognitive line at all, but in the cave of the heart, intuitively grasped as a whole new system of perceptivity.

There is a general, vague agreement that "nondual" has something to do with "no separation." But what does this mean exactly? Does it equate to a mystical experience ("Make me one with everything!"), a philosophical monism ("It's all one!"), a transcendence of polarity, or an elimination of polarity? Does it imply a permanent state of bliss or equanimity, or "merely"—as Bede Griffiths once famously suggested—the capacity to remain awake, present in *all* states? Can you still *think* in a nondual way, or is that an oxymoron? Is it the same thing as "permanent enlightenment"? The falling away of self? And if so, who would be the exemplars of this state in the Christian lineage? Is it the rare attainment of a saint, or an increasingly common phenomenon as civilization converges upon a new evolutionary leap?

I will attempt to sort out all this confusion a bit more methodically in part two. But in the swirl of these questions, I would simply like to announce here the criteria I am going to be using in this book, which will hopefully establish some concrete parameters around a notoriously elusive topic. This is in fact the "unifying thread" I alluded to in the opening paragraph. Here it is, explicitly stated:

Whatever nondual may look like when approached through the metaphysical and spiritual filters classically used to describe it, *neurologically, the capacity to perceive reality in this way depends on a new way of organizing the perceptual field*—an upgrade in the operating system, if you will. Basically, the essence of the nondual is a quantitative change not in the object of perception but in the *mechanics* of perception. Rather than "perception through differentiation" (the programming used by the cognitive mind), one begins to perceive through *holographic resonance*—the capacity to sense the whole pattern as a single unified field. Of course one then "sees *from* wholeness" (i.e., nonseparation).

As I try to unpack my perspective here, I will add to it two further corollaries:

First, the West's particular contribution to the understanding of nonduality has been, I believe, to intuit that this evolutionary advance is somehow connected to "putting the mind in the heart"—a phrase which leaps from page after page of Orthodox accounts of this transformation and is also detectable, though in more obscure form, in the mystical writings of the Christian West. While it is easy to dismiss this as simply a sentimental allusion to the fact that "feeling" is the catalytic element in transformation, recent discoveries in the field of neuroscience (which we will be looking at in due course) suggest that we might want to take a second look, with greater amenability to the possibility that these ancient monks actually knew more about the rewiring of consciousness than at first meets the eye.

And second, Centering Prayer has a very specific and substantial contribution to make to this rewiring of consciousness precisely in these "untraditional" aspects of its methodology, namely, its cultivation of a foundational capacity for attention of the heart and objectless awareness.

The book will unfold in three sections, each with its own specific contribution to make to the overall game plan. Part one may strike you as deceptively breezy—and in a way it is, for it was originally constructed as a beginner's course in Centering Prayer that ran on the Spirituality and Practice website in 2011 (and is still available there as an online self-study program). Even if you consider yourself an old hand at Centering Prayer, I encourage you not to skip over this section, for you'll see that I do a few things distinctly differently here from the standard methodology of a Contemplative Outreach introductory workshop. In particular, my emphasis on the releasing of thoughts as a preliminary exercise in objectless awareness is foundational to all that follows in this book and is most likely new territory for most of you.

In part two, I will begin to paint the wider picture, fleshing out some of the pieces I've alluded to in this introductory overview. You'll find more on what I mean by nondual consciousness as an "operating system." And we'll spend considerable time exploring those teachings on attention of the heart and the means by which this attention is engaged. I will also have a few things to say about those standard items in any consideration of the nondual—namely, witnessing presence and the transcendence of egoic selfhood—as they play out in Centering Prayer.

Part three is essentially an extended commentary on the first third of that fourteenth-century spiritual classic *The Cloud of Unknowing*, familiar to most Centering Prayer practitioners as the immediate source of Centering Prayer. This section began life as a keynote presentation delivered at the annual conference of Contemplative Outreach of Colorado in March 2013 and has undergone extensive revision, which in the process has taken me back to my earliest (pre–Centering Prayer and preordination) career as a scholar and medievalist. It has been a rewarding reunion of these two deep rivers of my life.

While *The Cloud* is superficially familiar to most Christian practitioners, it remains difficult and intimidating to many, and for good reason. Because of its insistence that "God may be reached and held close by means of love, but by means of thought never,"[2] it is usually categorized as a specimen of Christian affective mysticism. And yet it quickly becomes apparent that neither "love" nor "thought" actually mean what they might at first appear to, and that the more we try to apply the terms in the familiar way, the more frustrating and self-canceling the instructions become.

I will propose to break open *The Cloud* through the lens of "objectless awareness," that unnamed but obliquely recognized quality I referred to earlier in this introduction. Rather than as a typical exemplar of "Christian love mysticism," I see this text as the earliest Christian exploration of the phenomenology of consciousness, its anonymous author clearly on the trail of a different way of configuring the attentional field as the key element in unlocking a whole different kind of perceptivity, which he astonishingly equates with *contemplation*. If he's right here, he may in fact be naming the closest point of equivalency between traditional Christian formulations and our contemporary understanding of the nondual. We will hold that possibility open as we circle in for a closer look.

As a thirty-year practitioner of Centering Prayer, I am by no means blind to its rough edges or predictable stuck places, many of which emerge precisely from that innovative move of Keating, already mentioned, to bypass the usual starting points assumed in most traditional meditational practices: focused attention, breath, embodiment. It's true that daydreaming is an occupational hazard of this method of meditation, and that a lot of practitioners still get tangled up in self-reflection and a confused understanding of the sacred word, wobbling somewhere between a mantra and minesweeper. These are operational difficulties that will need to be addressed more fully by an upcoming generation of Centering

Prayer teachers—and in fact are already being addressed, most forcefully by Keating's longtime student and protégé, David Frenette.[3]

But neither do I think that Centering Prayer is a flawed method or a "spiritual lightweight," as some recent commentators have less than charitably implied. More than anything else, I continue to be impressed by Centering Prayer's fidelity to the heart of the Christian tradition and its ability, when explicitly moored in this tradition, to lead its practitioners toward nondual awakening along a pathway that corresponds to authentically Christian and Western reference points. Implicit in this statement, of course, is, as a kind of subtext for those "with ears to hear," that the standards and metaphysical road maps used to sketch our present understanding of the nondual often do not do full credit to the extent and sophistication of the Christian understanding of this tradition, as well as the distinctive metaphysical backdrop against which it unfolds. Using Centering Prayer to help the one leverage the other, I hope in the long run to contribute to the evolving dialogue on this subject.

PART ONE

A Short Course *on* Centering Prayer

Overview

As I mentioned in the introduction, this first section of my book began as a monthlong online e-course offered on the Spirituality and Practice website in fall 2011. In its original format the course consisted of a short lesson, an accompanying spiritual practice, additional written and audio resource materials, and an online forum where students could exchange observations and questions. This present, somewhat condensed, version consists of the eight original lessons only, slightly modified to remove specific references to the e-course and to connect more directly with the material under exploration in this book. I have decided to retain the somewhat informal and conversational tone, as it is an essential ingredient in the overall impact of the presentation.

For those of you who know Centering Prayer only by hearsay, I hope you will take the time to familiarize yourself with this section—and most important, actually try out the practice! As will most likely become apparent, Centering Prayer is a good deal more nuanced than it at first appears, and many of the misconceptions that continue to circulate about this practice are caused by a too hasty assumption that Centering Prayer is simply a Christianized version of some generic mindfulness practice. It manifestly is not, and it's precisely in these

divergences that its real integrity as a method shines through—
and the material which will make up this book is to be located.
If you think that Centering Prayer is like any other method
of meditation, you won't have a clue where I'm coming from
when I start to talk about objectless awareness and attention
of the heart. So take the time to work with these eight lessons,
assimilate Centering Prayer's somewhat unique methodology,
and see what the practice actually feels like from the meditation cushion. I guarantee that the time so invested will make
everything clearer.

Even if you're an old hand at Centering Prayer, I still encourage you not to skip over these lessons. While my understanding of Centering Prayer predominantly follows the main
course of the teaching developed by Contemplative Outreach
over these past three decades, there are places where my
emphasis is distinctly different, particularly around the understanding of the sacred word, *kenosis* as key to everything, and
attention of the heart, which is close but not identical to the
"heartfulness" teaching presently promulgated throughout the
Centering Prayer network. In general, my approach is probably more phenomenological than you're used to (tied to what
is actually happening in the moment rather than theological
constructs) and more interspiritually oriented than the normal
instructional format, as I am seeking specifically to dialogue
with an audience larger than just practicing Christians. So
even if you're familiar with the standard presentation (and
perhaps have taught it yourself hundreds of times!), it's still
worth checking out the subtly different flavor of my take on
Centering Prayer. And once again, this is where many of the
new insights emerge from.

The material is intended to be basic and user-friendly, so
enjoy the ride! But I trust you'll see quickly that the concepts
being introduced here are anything but elementary. Rather,
they are the core building blocks of a whole new mode of per-

ception, nowadays widely known as "the nondual," which has been lying there right beneath our noses, largely unsuspected, since the earliest days of Centering Prayer. Simple though these lessons may be, I have tried to arrange the contents so that these building blocks become clearer, because they are what this book is really all about.

LESSON 1

Getting (Re)oriented

Learning Centering Prayer begins with *unlearning* most of what you think meditation is all about:

- Centering Prayer is not about attaining a state of bliss, peace, or stillness.
- It's not about developing "single-pointed concentration."
- It's not about establishing a steady "I am" or witnessing presence.
- It's not about reducing stress or improving physical or emotional wellness (although these are indeed common side effects).
- It's not about receiving messages from God.

What *is* it about, then?

Basically, the method of Centering Prayer consists in learning to withdraw attention from our thoughts—those incessant creations of our busy minds—in order to rest in a gentle, open attentiveness to divine reality itself. This gentle releasing of thoughts is known in Centering Prayer teaching as "consenting to the presence and action of God." It is not hard to do, but it's hard—at first—to value.

In Centering Prayer, a thought is defined as *anything that brings your attention to a focal point.* It can be an idea, but it can also be a vision, a memory, an emotion, or even an itch on your nose. If it captures your attention, it's a thought, and the basic instruction is simply to let it go, gently releasing it from the grip of your attention. If another thought pops right back up to take its place, that's quite all right; let it go, too.

So am I really saying that in Centering Prayer you meditate by simply letting go of one thought after another? That can certainly be our subjective experience of the practice, and this is exactly the frustration expressed by an early practitioner of this prayer in a story now quite famous in the annals of Centering Prayer. In one of the very earliest training workshops led by Father Thomas Keating himself, a nun tried out her first twenty-minute taste of Centering Prayer and then lamented, "Oh, Father Thomas, I'm such a failure at this prayer. In twenty minutes I've had ten thousand thoughts!"

"How lovely," responded Keating, without missing a beat. "Ten thousand opportunities to return to God."

This simple story captures the essence of Centering Prayer. It is quintessentially *a pathway of return* in which every time the mind is released from engagement with a specific idea or impression, we move from a smaller and more constricted state of consciousness into that open, diffuse awareness in which our presence to divine reality makes itself known along a whole different pathway of perception. That's what the author of the fourteenth-century spiritual classic *The Cloud of Unknowing* may have had in mind when he said, "God can be held fast and loved by means of love, but by thought never." "Love" is this author's pet word for that open, diffuse awareness, which gradually allows another and deeper way of knowing to suffuse one's entire being. (We will be meeting *The Cloud of Unknowing* in far greater depth in part three of this book.)

It's a little bit like learning to see in the dark. Our normal daytime vision relies primarily on the cones: photoreceptors in the eye that are highly attuned to light, to sharp focus, and to acute differentiation. As the daylight fades, we rely more and more on our rods, which perceive peripherally, taking in the whole pattern through the gloom and subtle presence of the landscape. I have always considered it a fine piece of synchronicity that the normal length of time required for our day vision to give way to night vision—twenty minutes—is exactly the length of time recommended for a period of Centering Prayer.

In the language of Contemplative Outreach, the membership network founded by Thomas Keating to promote the practice of Centering Prayer, this letting go of thoughts is seen as "consenting to the presence and action of God." It carries that core sense of "Not my will but thine be done, O Lord," the words uttered by Jesus in the garden of Gethsemane on the night before his crucifixion. Every time we're willing to let go of our engagement with a thought, no matter how captivating, and return to that simple, open-ended awareness, we are in spirit participating—in solidarity with Christ—in that great gesture of self-surrender through which the world was redeemed. This traditional devotional understanding may or may not appeal to you, but there is also some very interesting confirmation emerging from recent neuroscience to suggest that learning to let go of what we're clinging to, mentally as well as emotionally, does indeed catalyze some revolutionary—and evolutionary—changes in our neural wiring. We'll be looking at some of that fascinating research a bit later in this series of lessons.

When I've talked with people who report difficulty in getting a practice of Centering Prayer off the ground, in virtually every case the problem turns out to be that they're overcomplicating it. The challenge in Centering Prayer is not because it's difficult but because it's so very, very simple. "Ten thousand opportunities to return to God": if you can just keep that in your head, the rest of the picture will gradually fill in.

The immediate implications of this simplicity are as follows:

First, as you sit down to do this practice, you don't need to focus on pushing away thoughts or keeping them from emerging in the first place. The work of Centering Prayer is not done on the "front end": in your ability to access and sustain a state of openness or stillness. The work is done on the "back end," in the exact moment when you realize that you've gotten engaged with a thought and are willing to let the thought go. It's your willingness, plus the subtle but real shift in the energy field of your attention when you release it from its object, that does the trick.

Second, this means that Centering Prayer is a total "win-win" practice. Whatever happens to you during a meditation period is just fine. If you settle down on your chair or prayer stool and immediately fall into twenty minutes of deep stillness, great! You've had a profound spiritual rest. If you sit there and every minute of the twenty minutes feels like twenty minutes, your mind dogged with thoughts, but you're still doing the best you can to let them go, that's fine, too! You've gotten a great aerobic workout for your "muscle" of consent.

Later on in these lessons you'll see that I am not just speaking figuratively here. For now, I'd simply like to plant the idea that *the real work of Centering Prayer is to lay the inner foundations for an entirely different kind of spiritual attentiveness.* It doesn't work with that sharp clarity of the mind prized in so many meditational paths, nor with a force-ful single-pointedness of the will. Later we will see why it is indeed appropriate to name this pathway of perception that Centering opens up "attention of the heart." It will gradually lead you into a whole new reality, which some have likened to "putting on the mind of Christ."

In the next lesson, we'll fine-tune the distinction between attention and intention and begin to work through the specific

steps in the method itself. But as you embark on this new
learning curve, it's important to keep the big picture in mind,
so that you don't waste a lot of time working against yourself or looking for results in the wrong places. You will come
to deeper spiritual attentiveness, certainly, but by Centering
Prayer's own unique route.

LESSON 2

Intention Is Everything

"Centering Prayer is done not with attention but with *intention*," Keating repeatedly reminds his aspiring practitioners.
Unlike other methods of meditation, Centering Prayer does
not furnish an object for your attention—whether it be by
repeating a mantra, following your breath, or watching your
thoughts as they arise. Rather, you simply withdraw your
attention from anything that brings it to a focal point and
return again and again to your underlying intention—what
The Cloud of Unknowing calls your "naked intent direct to
God."

In Centering Prayer, then, everything begins with and keeps
returning to intention. What am I really up to in this prayer?
What is my aim as I sit down on my chair or prayer stool and
set this practice in motion?

It's difficult, admittedly, to put words around an experience
that is deeply personal and intuitive. But in general, you're in
the right ballpark if your intention is "to be totally open to
God": totally available, all the way down to that innermost
point of your being; deeper than your thinking, deeper than
your feelings, deeper than your memories and desires, deeper
than your usual psychological sense of yourself. Ultimately,
what will go on in this prayer is "in secret" (the words that
Jesus used in his instructions on prayer in Matthew 6:6):

hidden even from yourself, in that innermost sanctuary of your being—where, in the words of that well-loved Christian monastic formula, your life is "hidden with Christ in God."

PUTTING TEETH IN YOUR INTENTION

"The road to hell is paved with good intentions." This familiar aphorism aptly describes the experience of nearly everyone who begins to work with Centering Prayer. You'll sit down on your cushion or prayer stool with the lofty intention of making yourself totally available to God, and not twenty seconds later you'll find yourself deeply embroiled in some mental or emotional scenario: replaying that argument you had with your boss yesterday or wondering what to cook for dinner tonight. Ah, monkey mind, as the Buddhists call it! And you'll wonder what ever became of that "naked intent direct to God."

The method of Centering Prayer begins with the reassurance that this is all perfectly normal. Rather than trying to access or maintain a steady state of concentration, Centering Prayer proposes a simple and elegant solution to the problem of monkey mind. You might think of it in terms of a little "deal" that you make with yourself. The deal is this: *if you catch yourself thinking, you let the thought go.*

It's as simple as that. You're not responsible for the thoughts you don't catch (at least not at first—I'll offer some refinements to this instruction a bit later). And you don't need to torment yourself with the question of "Who or what 'catches itself' thinking?" Just deal with what's on your plate, which will be more than enough to keep you busy. If you find yourself tangled up with a thought—no matter what kind of thought—you simply, gently let that thought go. You release it, thus bringing yourself back into alignment with your original intention, which was to maintain that bare, formless openness to God.

Of course, the next thought may be right back, reducing the duration of your bare, formless openness to a nanosecond. No problem—just let that thought go, as well. The essence of this method lies in the prompt *releasing* of thoughts, not in stopping them from arising in the first place. Remember, "Ten thousand opportunities to return to God!"

LESSON 3

Choosing a Sacred Word

If you've made it this far in the instructions, you've basically learned the method of Centering Prayer. But to make the method a bit easier to apply, a finishing touch is added. In Centering Prayer, this release of a thought is normally accomplished with the help of something known as a *sacred word*.

Oh, you mean a mantra? No. A mantra is a word you repeat constantly throughout the meditation as a touchstone for your attention. A sacred word merely serves as a placeholder for your intention. It's the spiritual equivalent of a little piece of red string tied around your finger to remind yourself of your willingness to "do the deal." Unlike a mantra, you don't repeat it constantly; you only use it when you realize you've gotten tangled up in a thought. Then it helps gently and quickly to clear the mental debris and return you to that bare, open awareness. In Centering Prayer, this gentle release of your thoughts is seen as "consenting to God's presence and action within."

When you're first learning Centering Prayer, the distinction may appear academic—it may seem that you're mostly dropping one thought after another, so the sacred word might *as well* be a mantra. But in fact, even in your earliest attempts at this prayer, there will be "gaps": places where thinking drops out and the word drops out, and you're simply there—traveling at the speed of love, as I like to picture it. It's in these gaps that Centering Prayer does its real transformative work.

The basic strategy behind the sacred word goes all the way back to the origin of Centering Prayer in *The Cloud of Unknowing*. There, in chapter 7, its anonymous author writes:

> For this reason, whenever you feel yourself drawn to devote yourself to this work [of contemplative prayer] . . . a naked intent direct to God is sufficient without anything else.
>
> And if you desire to have this aim concentrated and expressed in one word in order that you may be better able to grasp it, take but one short word of a single syllable. This is better than two, for the shorter it is the better it accords with the spirit. Such a word is the word GOD or the word LOVE. Choose whichever one you prefer, or, if you like, choose another that suits your taste, provided that it is one syllable. And clasp this word tightly in your heart so that it never leaves it no matter what may happen.[1]

Note that despite the *Cloud* author's firm insistence that the word in question must be no more than one syllable, it has always been perfectly permissible in Centering Prayer teaching to use a two- or three-syllable word, or even a short phrase, provided that it is *very* short—like "Let go" or "Be still." Anything more elaborate tends to stimulate conceptual thinking: exactly the opposite of what you're trying to do.

In many meditation paths a mantra is simply given to you by your spiritual teacher. But in Centering Prayer you get to choose, for as the instructions emphasize, it's your *intention* that makes your sacred word sacred, rather than any inherent devotional or vibrational content. As you make your choice, here are some guidelines to keep in mind:

• Some people are more comfortable with traditional religious words—like "God" or "Abba" or "Jesus" or "Spirit" or short phrases like "Come, Lord." Others prefer what I call "state" words that remind you of that open availability you want to keep returning to: words like "peace," "open," "let go," "yes." Either kind is perfectly fine.

• Your word should be as emotionally neutral as possible. Remember, it serves only as a placeholder for your intention. If you make it too special—"my precious love word for God!"—it may have too much emotional or conceptual weight on it, which will tend to stimulate thinking rather than reduce it.

• Most people "shop around" for a word quite a bit during their early days of learning Centering Prayer. That's perfectly normal. Often when the right word comes, it's with a force and resonance so strong that one can hardly avoid suspecting the Holy Spirit as the chief operative. One woman I know went back and forth for several sessions between "trust" and "love." Finally, she watched in astonishment as they fused themselves into a short phrase, "trust love," which has been her sacred word ever since.

• The only unbreakable rule is this: don't shop for your word within the prayer period itself. The reason is pretty obvious: then you'd be thinking!

• Once your word arrives, it's good to consider it a long-term engagement. I've had mine for more than twenty years now. Over time your word imprints itself deeply in your unconscious, the place from which it really does its work. Not only will it help jog your memory during the meditation period itself, it will even begin to show up out of the meditation time when you're poised on the edge of reactivity or stress, gently reminding you that "the presence and action of God within" is not something that disappears when you get up from your meditation cushion.

• Your sacred word is not secret, but nor is it a subject for chatter and gossip. It is, after all, the symbol of your "intention to consent to God's presence and action within," and that gives it a serious and sacred intentionality. Be respectful of it and the work it does.

DOES IT HAVE TO BE A WORD?

Centering Prayer teaching allows people, if they're so inclined, to substitute a "sacred glance" or a "sacred breath" for the sacred word. I admit that I have always been slightly uncomfortable with this suggestion, however. The risk in using a sacred glance (which used to be called a "sacred image," a visual symbol instead of a word) is that you start visualizing. The risk in using the breath is that it will pull you into *following* the breath, using it like a mantra as a touchstone for your attention. Visualization and following the breath are both classic methods of meditation, but they are not Centering Prayer. If you do opt for either of these alternatives, remember that your "sacred glance" or "sacred breath" must be used exactly like the sacred word: merely as a placeholder for your intention.

LESSON 4

The Mechanics of Sitting

Despite first appearances, meditation is not an out-of-body experience. You are not escaping from your physicality to enter some formless spiritual world. Everything that happens to you in meditation actually happens in and through your body; in some ways this is even truer in Centering Prayer than on other meditation paths. So it is important to give the body its due and to treat it with respect and dignity as you sit, both inwardly and outwardly.

In Centering Prayer the goal is to keep the body relaxed

but alert. You want to keep it as neutral as possible so that it doesn't get in the way, either by calling attention to itself or by falling asleep.

As in all meditation, it's good to have your back as straight as possible and your head balanced on your shoulders, neither drooping down nor scrunched up. (Those are great ways to give yourself a splitting headache!) Basically, this is the same position you'd be aiming for if you were singing in a choir. It allows the best conditions for staying present and attentive and for allowing your energy to circulate freely within you.

This being said, "relaxed but alert" is always measured against the yardstick of your own physical capacity. If you need to prop yourself up to support your back or sit in an overstuffed chair to cushion aching muscles, by all means do so. I've seen many people with back problems do Centering Prayer lying flat on their backs.

It doesn't matter whether you sit in a chair or on a cushion or prayer stool; it's your choice. Unless you're accustomed to sitting in lotus position, don't cross your legs: it impedes the circulation of energy within you (and is often connected to an attitude as well!). If you're short and have opted for the chair, a small stool or pillow under your feet helps you keep your knees comfortably horizontal. If you've opted for the floor, a good way to keep your legs from falling asleep is to make sure that your buttocks are always higher than your knees. Your hands rest comfortably on your knees, either palms down or palms up.

Typically your eyes are closed. In Centering Prayer teaching this is understood as part of the "consent to the presence and action of God" by letting go of what is going on around and within you. But common sense prevails here; if you find yourself falling asleep, open your eyes and bring them to a soft focus; it will bring you right back.

AH, "BROTHER ASS!"

"Brother Ass" is how Saint Francis often humorously referred to his body. And during the course of the prayer period, it's not at all uncommon for Brother Ass to kick back at you. Suddenly there will be an itch on your nose or a throat tickle or cough; sometimes a leg goes to sleep, or there may even be a sudden ache or cramp. Some of this (particularly any muscle tightness around the neck or upper back) can be caused by trying too hard—*Relax!*—but part of it is simply the way that Centering Prayer does its work. During our busy outer lives we often hold ourselves in overly tense or stained positions, and our inner parts take up the slack. In the deep relaxation of Centering Prayer (which Thomas Keating likens to "taking a brief vacation from yourself"), the overly tensed parts have a chance to unkink. Knots of pain or tension we carry unconsciously in our bodies can all of a sudden loosen up. This is good news for the body, but often uncomfortable and even embarrassing in the prayer, particularly if you're doing it in a group.

People often wonder how best to deal with these physical intrusions. Should I treat this itch or cough like a thought and try to let it go? Should I bring my attention directly to it for a few moments until it subsides? Or should I just cough or shift my body posture and be done with it? Avowed hedonist that I am, I usually opt for this third route. Why spend a whole prayer period in agony trying to not think about needing to cough when a few seconds of coughing will put the whole episode behind you? Admittedly, when you're meditating in a group, there needs to be some external consideration here. For the sake of the overall silence, it's important to try not to fidget or to engage in prolonged physical behaviors (coughing, weeping, heavy breathing) that might disturb others around you. It's perfectly all right to simply leave the room quietly and go settle yourself down.

BECOMING AN ICON OF PRAYER

Yes, *of course,* Centering Prayer is an inward experience, not an outer performance. But there is still a certain yoga to it that has been consistently underemphasized in the teaching to date. When you sit in meditation, you are actually presenting yourself as an icon of one of the most archetypal and noble of human activities: communion with the infinite. Being aware of the natural dignity and beauty of this archetype will help your own body find its place more easily, and it will also be of substantial help to everybody else when you meditate in a group.

LESSON 5

Putting It All Together

So what does a period of Centering Prayer actually look like? Now that we've worked through the most important details individually, it's time to put the whole package together.

If you're an old hand at Centering Prayer, of course, this will all be familiar territory; you've probably done this drill hundreds, maybe even thousands, of times! But there are always those nuances to be fine-tuned, and hearing even familiar instructions from a new perspective can sometimes lead to unexpected insights. So let's do a brief walk-through.

You begin by sitting down in your chair or on your prayer stool or cushion: eyes closed, body relaxed but alert. If you wish, you can collect yourself around your intention with a short prayer such as "Into your hands I commend my spirit," or "O God, I am here; O God, you are here," or by taking a couple of intentional breaths. But Centering Prayer actually begins when you start to "say" your sacred word, offering it silently, gently, and at first steadily as a symbol of your willingness to consent to the presence and action of God during this prayer time.

The next step is the most important in the practice, and also the most difficult to explain. For a time, during the early days of Centering Prayer teaching, the instruction used to go something like this: "When you notice you're no longer being attracted to thinking, it's okay to let your sacred word go . . ."

But of course, these instructions are self-canceling and have been the bane of many practitioners attempting to get the hang of this prayer. How can you "notice" without thinking? How can you "decide" to let the word go without that itself being a thought?

In reality, however, there is a simple magic here, again dependent on that wonderful operative we already touched on in our earlier discussion of the sacred word: the participation of your unconscious. The easiest way to describe what happens might be through a kind of butchered French, "*il se droppe*"—the word simply drops itself out. It's very similar to the process of falling asleep. You can't see the moment you actually drift off to sleep. It simply happens.

It's essentially the same in Centering Prayer. The crucial moment is taken care of. You don't have to "do" it; it happens on its own, programmed right into your original intention to be deeply open to God. You won't notice the moment you stop thinking; what you'll notice is the moment you *start* thinking again. You find yourself in the midst of a thought and return to your sacred word as a way of returning to that openness. And then another thought comes, and with it, another return to the sacred word—"ten thousand opportunities to return to God."

And on and on it goes, for the twenty minutes or so that you do this prayer. It has sort of a sine-wave pattern: rhythmically up and down. Subjectively, the only parts you'll directly re-member are the times of wrestling with your thoughts. But in point of fact, these relatively more agitated, "surface of your-self" times have been counterbalanced by times of deep resting at your depths. You won't be able to perceive these directly of course; the moment you start thinking about them, they're gone. But you'll retain some residual memory of them in an inexplicable sense of refreshment, and sometimes a vivid sense of having been tugged down deep into your own heart, or having sat at the edge of an incredible intimacy and tenderness.

Both of which are true, incidentally. During those nano-second gaps in the stream of consciousness, you have been resting in the river of "pure awareness," and it floods through your being like autumn rains after a long drought. Later, as your practice becomes more stable and you imprint deeply on your heart the know-how that the way to get there is to let go of what you're clinging to so that your attention relaxes from its default subject/object trajectory, then, bit by bit you'll discover that this inner spaciousness is no longer "a place you go to" but "a place you *come from*." It begins to offer itself as a new home for your deepest sense of selfhood.

These are very important observations, which are rarely mentioned in the main body of Centering Prayer teaching, and which, as you'll soon see, furnish the experiential foundation for most of what I will be up to in the rest of this book.

So that's about it for our walk-through: except to remind you once again to come out of Centering Prayer gently, allowing some time for your eyes to come from closed to a soft focus and to linger there in that soft focus for a minute or two before resuming the sharp-edged focus of the mind's usual way of paying attention. That way, you'll get to "keep" more of the interior spaciousness you've touched in Centering Prayer as you move about your day.

A FEW TIMEKEEPING ISSUES

The standard time prescription for establishing a Centering Prayer practice is "twenty minutes, twice a day." This has been the entry-level commitment recommended by Thomas Keating and Contemplative Outreach for more than thirty years, and it has successfully launched tens of thousands of people on their journeys. I am sometimes asked whether it is all right to do just one prayer period a day, and while this is a definite "no-no" in the official teachings of Centering Prayer, I myself prefer to err on the side of leniency. Two is definitely preferable, but if one is all you can see your way clear to at the start, I'd rather see you get one up and running than abandon the whole project because you can't fit in two.

An obvious question: how do I know when the twenty minutes of meditation is over? You can certainly set a watch or a timer. (There are now some lovely chime ring tones available that won't drive you straight to the ceiling when the timer goes off.) For myself, however, I simply glance occasionally at my watch. The attentional pattern in Centering Prayer is up and down anyway, and if you do happen to get caught in rapt attentiveness and stay a little beyond the appointed twenty minutes, what harm is done?

In general, however, it's best to stick to the appointed twenty minutes, ending at the designated time. This maintains a certain objectivity in the practice that cuts through the temptation to lengthen or shorten the prayer period according to your subjective experience of how it is going. The "I feel really gathered and deep; I think I'll sit for longer today" can easily be counterbalanced by the "I'm really restless today; I think I'll stop sooner"—and it's precisely in the pushing through that restlessness that the most important inner work is often done.

CENTERING PRAYER:
THE "OFFICIAL" GUIDELINES

For nearly thirty years now, these same basic points have been covered in Centering Prayer teaching in the form of four guidelines, which have successfully introduced tens of thousands of people worldwide to the practice. Old hands to Centering Prayer will already know these guidelines well, but if you're learning it here for the first time, you'll see that they furnish a concise summary of the ground we've covered so far from a slightly different angle of approach. Read over them carefully, and reflect on how they fit together with the material as I've presented it—and also with your own experience of this prayer now that you've had a chance to practice it straight through:

1. Choose a sacred word as the symbol of your willingness to consent to God's presence and action within.
2. Sitting comfortably and with eyes closed, settle briefly and silently introduce the sacred word as the symbol of your consent to God's presence and action within.
3. When engaged with your thoughts, return ever so gently to the sacred word.
4. At the end of the prayer period, remain in silence with eyes closed for a couple of minutes.

LESSON 6

Handling Thoughts during Centering Prayer

Now that you've all had your first "official" walk-through of Centering Prayer, it's time to return to the question of handling thoughts during the prayer period, since you now have a lot more data to work with. While "ten thousand opportunities to return to God" continues to be a familiar refrain, it's important to keep reminding yourself that thoughts are not an obstacle in Centering Prayer, but an *opportunity*. Each new thought gives you chance to exercise that "muscle" of letting go.

In this lesson I'd like to review some of the standard teaching in Centering Prayer circles about handling thoughts during prayer time, and then add a couple of insights of my own.

The first and most important thing to keep in mind is that the goal in Centering Prayer is not to stop thoughts altogether, *but to develop a detached attitude toward them.* Fighting your thoughts is useless; releasing them is blessed.

In one of his most colorful teachings, Thomas Keating describes this process using the metaphor of boats on a river. The river, as he depicts it, is your consciousness—which is in fact a constantly moving stream. Down it float boats—that is, your thoughts. They may be innocent little "kayaks," like a sudden wondering whether you left the keys in the car or if tomorrow is the day to put out the trash. Or they may be huge battleships of raw emotion and contentiousness, like reliving the fight you had with your boss last week. Or they may be half-sunken, waterlogged hulls barely above the surface: old hurts and memories from the past. On and on down the river they float.

According to this metaphor, the ideal way to position yourself during Centering Prayer is to imagine yourself as a scuba diver seated on a rock at the bottom of the riverbed. From your watery perch you can look up and see the boat hulls passing overhead. As long as they're passing by, that's fine. You don't have to do anything to prevent their coming and going.

The temptation, however, is to get interested in a particular boat, swim up to the surface, and climb on board. In other words, you get caught up in a particular thought. In place of that relaxed, detached attitude that lets the boats come and go, you are now being carried downstream yourself!

In Centering Prayer, you recall, a thought is not just an idea; it's anything that draws your attention to a focal point. It can be an emotion, a memory, an interior dialogue, a vision, or, just as easily, some physical distraction like the buzz of a fluorescent light overhead or a sudden pain in your back. *It's the configuration of your attention, not the content of the thought, that is the determining factor.*

This is an important distinction to keep in mind, for otherwise it's hard to avoid falling into the trap of judging your thoughts, chasing away the ones that seem random, negative, or "unspiritual," but lingering on those that seem holy or inspirational. The entire Judeo-Christian tradition predisposes us to viewing silence as the place par excellence for receiving messages from God, and it's very hard to break this well-engrained habit.

So here's a tough one: suppose, going back to that metaphor of boats on the river, you were suddenly to see amid the flotilla Jesus Christ himself calmly walking toward you on the water, smiling as he reaches forth his hand. The mystical brass ring! What do you do now? Put Centering Prayer on pause and grab it, right?

Wrong. The instructions remain the same. "If you catch yourself thinking, you let the thought go."

Ouch!

Centering Prayer teaching is quite correct in sticking to its guns here, however, and once you see the real rationale behind this teaching, it may be easier to get with the program. Basically, it all comes down to your attention again. The moment you take the bait and grab onto one of those juicy insights or tantalizing visions, your attention goes right back into subject/object mode, the default position of your mental-egoic mind. It's business as usual, the mind simply doing its thing, handing you reality through its built-in bifocal lens.

In those deeper waters of Centering Prayer, you are slowly acclimating to a whole new operating system: one that does not need to split the perceptual field in order to perceive. Think of it as an upgrade for your brain, if you like, but one way or another it will gradually help lay the physiological foundations for what's known as nondual (or unitive) consciousness. Being able to hold your attention as a tensile field of awareness (I love a Rumi metaphor for this: "quivering like a drop of mercury") is a key piece of this "rewiring" of consciousness, and in Centering Prayer, that's exactly what you're practicing!

So not taking the bait, even if the bait is overwhelmingly tempting, is way more important than it looks. Mystical visions, spiritual consolations, and tantalizing insights all come and go regularly on the spiritual path. But once you have learned to rest in that undivided sphere of perception, your whole life, both inner and outer, begins to shift subtly but irreversibly. Radiance and grace are no longer extraordinary events, but simply the ordinary atmosphere of the love you are beginning to indwell.

That's why Keating can say (with that signature twinkle in his eye), "If the Blessed Virgin herself should come up to you during meditation and offer to pluck a thorn from your flesh, the answer is 'Not now, dearie, I'm doing my Centering Prayer.'"

"THE FOUR R'S"

In introductory Centering Prayer workshops, this gentle, laissez-faire attitude toward thoughts is reinforced through a simple formula called "the four R's":

Resist no thought.
Retain no thought.
React to no thought.
Return ever so gently to the sacred word.

As you continue with your Centering Prayer practice, see if this formula helps you to release your thoughts more promptly and gently, and remembering always: "ten thousand opportunities to return to God!"

LESSON 7

Putting on the Mind of Christ

I have worked in interspiritual circles long enough to know that authentic spiritual practices are pretty much universal. For almost any practice in any tradition, you'll find its counterpart in another tradition if you know where to look. That's because the recipe for spiritual transformation is basically the same all over: surrender, attention, compassion. One way or another, you will pass through the same eye of the needle no matter what path you're on.

Yet Centering Prayer does have aspects that link it closely to its Christian roots and milieu. I won't say that comparable practices don't exist in other traditions; they do. But with Christianity there is a special affinity. I've come to believe that Centering Prayer's unusual methodology makes complete sense only within a Christian theological frame of reference. And vice versa: its simple but powerful pathway of transformation illumines better than any other practice I've ever tried what it means to "put on the mind of Christ."

It was ten years into my practice before I realized that the theological basis for Centering Prayer lies in the principle of kenosis, Jesus's self-emptying love that forms the core of his own self-understanding and life practice. (Why didn't anyone ever tell me that?) Saint Paul explains this principle by way of his beautiful hymn in Philippians 2:6–11, prefacing his comments by saying, "Let the same mind be in you that was in Christ Jesus":

> Though his state was that of God,
> yet he did not deem equality with God
> something he should cling to.
>
> Rather he emptied himself,
> and assuming the state of a slave,
> he was born in human likeness . . .

The phrase "emptied himself" in line 4 is the English translation of the Greek verb *kenosein,* which is where the word *kenosis* comes from. In context, you'll see exactly what it means: it's the opposite of the word "cling" in line 3. Jesus is practicing gentle release. And he continues to practice it in every moment of his life, as the next verse of the hymn (Philippians 2:8) makes clear:

> He being known as one of us
> humbled himself obedient unto death,
> even death on a cross.

How beautifully simple—the path of Jesus hidden right there in plain sight! While some Christians are still reluctant to think of Jesus as teaching a path (isn't it enough simply to be the Son of God?), in fact, the gospels themselves make clear that he is specifically inviting us to this journey and modeling how to do it. Once you see this, it's the touchstone throughout all his teaching: Let go! Don't cling! Don't hoard! Don't assert your importance! Don't fret. "Do not be afraid, little flock, it is your Father's good pleasure to give you the kingdom!" (Luke 12:32). And it's this same core gesture we practice in Centering Prayer: thought by thought by thought. You could really summarize Centering Prayer as *kenosis in meditation form*.

This is why the unique and somewhat counterintuitive methodology of Centering Prayer unlocks the heart of Christianity so well. Do you remember that very first lesson, where I said the most important thing in learning Centering Prayer is to forget everything you think you know about meditation? Centering Prayer is not about developing concentration, attaining clear mind, conscious presence, a strong witnessing "I," some desired state. In Centering Prayer you merely practice and practice the core kenotic motion: "let go, make space, unclench"—thought by thought by thought.

Apart from this kenotic ground, the practice of Centering Prayer may not make full sense. In fact, criticism is sometimes leveled at it by those used to more concentrative methods of meditation, questioning the advisability of letting go of everything, including the "I am" presence and the sacred word. But when this instruction is understood not as the deliberate cultivation of an interior vacuum ("sinking mind," as it's sometimes called), but rather, as a willing divestment of all possessions even up to and including personal consciousness, its appropriateness becomes clear—and its ability to inform the Christian life, dazzling. Slowly, steadily, Centering Prayer patterns into its practitioners what I would call the quintessential Jesus response: the meeting of any and all life situations by the complete, free giving of oneself.

Fascinating confirmation that kenosis is indeed an evolutionary human pathway is emerging from—of all places—recent discoveries in neuroscience. From fMRI data collected primarily by the California-based HeartMath Institute, you can now verify chapter and verse that how you respond to a stimulus in the outer world determines which neural pathways will be activated in your brain, and between your brain and your heart. If you respond with any form of initial negativity (which translates physiologically as constriction)—freezing, bracing, clinging, clenching, and so on—the pathway illumined leads to your amygdala (or "reptilian brain," as it's familiarly known): that most primitive part of your hindbrain, which controls a repertory of highly energized fight-or-flight responses. If you can relax *into* a stimulus—opening, softening, yielding, releasing—the neural pathway leads through the more evolutionarily advanced parts of your forebrain and, surprisingly, brings brain and heart rhythms into entrainment.

So when I talked about exercising that "muscle" of letting go, you can see now that I wasn't simply using a metaphor. Every time we manage to let go of a thought in Centering

Prayer, "consenting to the presence and action of God within," the gesture is actually *physically embodied*. It's not just an attitude; something actually "drops and releases" in the solar plexus region of your body, a subtle but distinct form of interior relaxation. Your nerves and muscles are doing the same thing on a miniature scale as you did on a larger, outer scale when you practiced that "gentle release motion." And in time, this gentle and persistent "inner aerobics," undertaken under the specific banner of Centering Prayer and in solidarity with Jesus's own kenotic path, will gradually establish that "mind of Christ" within you as your own authentic self.

The word *metanoia*, frequently translated as "repent" (or "change the direction you're looking for happiness!"), literally means "go beyond the mind," or "go into the larger mind." Centering Prayer invites you to do just that.

LESSON 8

The Fruits of Centering Prayer

"The fruits of Centering Prayer are found in daily life." This well-worn refrain has been part of Centering Prayer introductory workshops from the beginning, and it's still one of the most valuable pieces of advice around. Over and over people are reminded not to look for signs that this prayer is working for them in their subjective experiences during the prayer period themselves (for of course, these would be thoughts, and you'd have to let go of them!). The place to look for results is in what happens *after* you get up from your meditation cushion.

As that gentle releasing motion you've practiced in Centering Prayer gradually works its way into your system, most people will typically begin to notice a greater spaciousness and flexibility in their daily life, and along with this an improvement in their personal relationships. (Often it's the people closest to you who pick up on these changes first.)

I still chuckle at the story shared by one of our original e-course participants when, one week into the course, she suddenly noticed a huge sculpture of an eagle in flight not fifty yards from the orthodontist's office where she'd been regularly taking her sons for several months. "Has that sculpture always been there?" she asked. Her younger son replied, "Mom, you haven't seen it because you're usually in a big hurry to get us here on time." A Centering Prayer classic—and after just a week of sitting!

Time does slow down as we stop trying to push the river. Another of my favorite "fruits of Centering Prayer" stories was shared by a fellow trainee in my own first Centering Prayer formation retreat more than a quarter century ago. A highly organized, "type A" professor of psychology, recently retired as department chair at a local university, she recounted how she had found an outlet for her energy by volunteering at the local homeless shelter. "Before starting Centering Prayer, I could process five clients an hour," she reported. "Now I can only process two."

"Slow down, smell the roses, take time to be with life!" That's the inner transformation Centering Prayer is supporting in you, not only emotionally but physiologically as well. The very fact that Centering Prayer sets no goals—other than deep, open availability to God's presence—and renews that availability simply through a gentle release of whatever you happen to be clinging onto at the moment gradually imprints the realization that this might just be a good way to do life, too!

HEALING THE UNCONSCIOUS

I don't mean to imply it's all a bed of roses however. Through the action of this same gentle releasing motion, it sometimes happens that painful material buried tightly in your unconscious can begin to respond to that invitation as well and surface into your consciousness during the time of the prayer in the form of painful memories, tears, or sudden emotional and physical pain.

Thomas Keating was one of the first contemporary spiritual teachers to name this process for what it is—a purification, or *healing*, of the unconscious—and the teachings he has built around this under the title "the divine therapy" are justly famous and have helped thousands of people weather the process. (Around the Centering Prayer network, this purification is often referred to more unceremoniously as "the unloading of the unconscious.")

Typically this won't happen to you until you're well established in your Centering Prayer practice, and even then, it usually only becomes really noticeable during immersion retreats, where you're doing three hours or more of Centering Prayer a day. At the recommended "dosage" of twenty minutes twice a day, this purification is more like a gentle scrubbing and does most of its work without your even noticing. Still, should this "unloading" happen to you, rest assured that it's all perfectly normal and try to treat it like any other thought that occurs during the prayer time: just let it go. There are plenty of resources available within the Contemplative Outreach network to help you understand this process better and work with it constructively. Remember, the end result is a markedly increased interior freedom and joy.

ATTENTION OF THE HEART

Perhaps the subtlest fruit of the practice (and the most delicious!) is a gradually deepening capacity to abide in the state of "attention of the heart," as it's known in the Christianity of the East. You might describe this as a stable state of mindfulness or "witnessing presence," but emanating from the heart, not the head, and thus free of intrusion from that heavy-handed mental "inner observer" who seems to separate us from the immediacy of our lives. The essence of this kind of attentiveness is perhaps best summed up in those words from the Song of Songs: "I sleep, but my heart is awake." Once you get the hang of it, attention of the heart allows you to be fully present to God, but at the same time fully present to the situation at hand, giving and taking from the spontaneity of your own authentic, surrendered presence.

Again, this kind of presence is a capacity that has been developing in you as you gradually learn in Centering Prayer to withdraw your attention from its default subject/object positioning and rest in that diffuse, objectless awareness. As this capacity grows in you, it gradually takes shape as a felt center of gravity within you, the place where the pendulum of your being naturally comes to rest. It's not so much a place you pay attention *to* as a place you pay attention *from*. But as you come to dwell there, life becomes seamlessly whole.

As I see it, the purpose of Centering Prayer is to deepen your relationship with God (and at the same time your own deepest self) in that bandwidth of formless, objectless awareness that is the foundation of nondual consciousness. There you discover that you, God, and the world "out there" are not separate entities, but flow together seamlessly in an unbreakable dynamism of self-giving love, which is the true nature of reality and the ground of everything. In that space you discover the meaning of Keating's famous statement "The notion that God is absent is the fundamental illusion of the human condition." And it is this track—Centering Prayer as both a foundation and an access route to the stabilization of nondual consciousness—that this book will now proceed to explore.

PART TWO

The Way
of the Heart

CHAPTER I

What Is Nonduality?

As you've probably noticed, "nondual" is one of the most eagerly sought after titles in the spiritual marketplace today, and to label anything "nondual" is to reinforce the powerful connotation that it's "good," "advanced," and "enlightened." But if you find yourself a bit confused about what nonduality actually means, you're not alone. Over the past few decades during which the term has snowballed its way to its current rock star status, it has accumulated such a retinue of overlapping and even competing meanings that it actually creates more confusion than enlightenment. To my way of thinking, "nondual" now rivals "soul" as a term whose meaning has become so vague and idiosyncratic that it might be better to declare a moratorium on its use until everyone can agree to at least a baseline definition.

A good deal of the confusion originates in the fact that the term *nonduality* is not a part of the innate vocabulary of the Christian spiritual tradition. It's what linguists would call a "loan word": a term imported specifically through contact with another language or culture—in this case, the metaphysical framework of the Eastern religions, which first became widely popular in the West during the second half of the twentieth century. Previous to this time, you won't find the term anywhere in the traditional vocabulary and mystical self-understanding of the West, which has conceived of the spiritual journey according to a very different road map. And so a good deal of the confusion has entered as folks have scrambled to catch up, to discover what, if anything, in our Western Christian experience most closely corresponds to what the East is intending by *nondual*. And as you might expect, it's a bit like the five blind men trying to describe an elephant.

Nonduality as Nonpolarization

Perhaps the simplest, most straightforward approach is exemplified by my colleague Richard Rohr, who uses the term *nondual* to designate one's personal capacity to bear paradox and ambiguity. According to his influential (and enormously practical) understanding, "dualistic" thinking is thinking marked by a rigorous "either/or" dichotomy and the insistence on black-and-white, exclusive solutions. "Nondual" is expressed in the capacity to hold the tension of opposites, rest comfortably in ambiguity, and resist the tendency to demonization and exclusion. It is, as Rohr rightly observes, a fundamental prerequisite for any kind of skillful prophetic work in today's pluralistic culture.

He's partially right here, of course: all rigid, exclusive thinking is by definition dualistic. But the opposite is not necessarily true: open, inclusive, paradox-tolerant thinking is not necessarily nondual, at least by the more rigorous cognitive standards from which the term originally derives. If you consult any of the popular maps of levels of consciousness (particularly Ken Wilber's, which closely follow his Eastern metaphysical sources), the capacity to bear paradox and ambiguity emerges at the *rational* stage—a good three or four levels below the technically nondual—and is in fact the hallmark of the pluralistic (or "green") level of consciousness, whose motto is "coexist."[1] The capacity to tolerate ambiguity certainly marks an evolution in basic psychological and moral development, but it does not in and of itself constitute evidence of a stable nondual attainment.

Nonduality as Mystical Experience

Another popular approach is to equate nonduality with a mystical experience—or with mystical experience in general. Again, this works in one direction but not the other. By definition all mystical experience is nondual. (Remember that old joke: "What did the mystic say to the hot-dog vendor?" "Make me one with everything!") And for sure, the classic descriptions of mystical experience inevitably feature that brief, overpowering sense of the boundaries dissolving and finding oneself at one with everything, whether it's "seeing heaven in a grain of sand" or realizing, as did Thomas Merton, in his overpowering epiphany on the corner of Fourth and Walnut in Louisville, that "I loved all these people, that they were mine and I theirs, that we could not be alien to one another even though we were total strangers."[2] The boundaries dissolve, the oneness flows in, and the world is bathed, for as long as the experience lasts, with the radiance of intrinsic wholeness.

The problem, however, is that most mystical experiences are temporary. They are "states," not "stages," of consciousness as Wilber helpfully delineates in his recent teachings on the subject.[3] And when the radiance fades—as it inevitably does—one is back in the same old heavy-edged world. More problematically, as Wilber again points out, a person will interpret these mystical intuitions of oneness according to the stage of consciousness he or she has stably attained. (Saint Paul is a classic example here, whose extraordinary presentiments of being "taken up into third heaven" coexist with his harshly dualistic moral pronouncements, such as "women should keep silent in the churches.") And since these mystical experiences are by definition *ec-static* (i.e., taking one outside oneself), they tend to create the impression that nondual is by nature blissful, exotic, or an "altered state of consciousness"—all of the above being categories that betray an "experience/experiencer" dichotomy still firmly in the driver's seat, and hence, alas, no nondual attainment.

Nonduality as Unitive Attainment

But what if these mystical experiences were to continue indefinitely and cast themselves as a permanent state of consciousness? Would that be nondual? This assumption seems to lie at the root of the third major approach: to see nondual as a contemporary "homeomorphic equivalent" (to use Raimon Panikkar's key term here[4]) for what Christian tradition has classically known as "the unitive state," the highest level of spiritual attainment according to the traditional tripartite road map of "purgative," "illuminative," and "unitive."[5] Again, there is considerable merit in this approach. Metaphysically they are parallels: nondual is the top of the Eastern map, unitive the top of the Western. Both traditions hint at a permanent, irreversible shift in the seat of selfhood and in the perceptual field that flows out from this new identity. The former, nucleated sense of selfhood dissolves, and in its place there arises a capacity to live a flowing, unboundaried life in which the person becomes "oned" with God (as Julian of Norwich famously expressed it) and oned with one's neighbor, flowing in the fundamental matrix of love without need for either edges or centers. "What if true persons are circles whose centers are nowhere and whose circumferences are everywhere, interpenetrating each other with an intimacy that we can scarcely imagine?" ponders contemporary Christian non-dual teacher Beatrice Bruteau in a marvelous evocation of this unitive flowingness.[6]

And yet, there remains a certain "forcing the fit" here, and with it an inadvertent blurring of the fundamentally different metaphysical character of these otherwise parallel "third tier" stages. In the East, the experience tends to be monistic, or what Wilber calls an "I/I" realization.[7] One discovers one's own deepest essence and nature as *identical* with that Oneness, that ground luminosity, that unitive field—"I am that." In the West, the unitive state is always looked upon as *relational:* a mystical marriage, in which one is fully joined to God in love, subsumed in God through that love. But one does not *become* God; and nondual realization is always one of union ("two become one"), not identity. This imparts a distinctly different feeling tone to the unitive experience of the West.

And it must also be said, quite frankly—again if we rely on the more rigorous criteria of the Eastern metaphysical models—that not all those whom Christianity would identify as having attained the unitive state thereby display the qualities of nondual consciousness. Certainly there are some who do—Meister Eckhart comes immediately to mind, together with Hadewijch of Antwerp, Marguerite of Porete, and perhaps in our own times Bernadette Roberts. But many retain a more affective and personal stance in which union with the divine beloved remains uppermost—rather than a transcendence of the subject/object polarity that creates lover and beloved in the first place. In one of her most trenchant insights, contemporary mystic Roberts points out that even John of the Cross, the Carmelite master who "wrote the book," so to speak, on Christian unitive attainment, does not fully traverse the unitive terrain to access what lies at its endpoint in the dissolution of that subject/object polarity.[8] While she adamantly resists the term nondual as meaningless within Christianity, that "unnamable" next step which she describes so unflinchingly in her *The Experience of No-Self* and *The Path to No-Self* corresponds much more closely to the threshold of what the East would call the authentic nondual than to anything commonly encountered in Western typologies of the unitive. In short, not all whom the West regards as having reached the unitive are also nondual thinkers. And odd as it may sound, not all who attain the nondual are automatically also masters of the unitive—for reasons which I hope will become clear to you in the course of this book.

Nonduality as a Shift in the Structure of Perception

This "close but not identical" affinity between Western unitive and Eastern nondual suggests that we look a little more closely at the *phenomenological* aspects of this transition—or in other words, what the structures of perception are actually doing beneath all the metaphysics and devotion. Clearly there is a big shift in perception that takes place between "dualistic" and "nondualistic" levels of consciousness, resulting in these signature experiences of oneness and an unboundaried, flowing sense of selfhood. But what if this shift is not primarily about *what* one sees but *how* one sees? That it betokens not so much a new level of conscious attainment as a permanent shift in the structure of consciousness itself—as it were, a rewiring of the "operating system"?

For better or worse, this is the avenue of approach I will be working with in this book. I find it useful because it lifts the discussion beyond the traditional interior and subjective (read "fuzzy") criteria used to measure nondual attainment ("How do you know if you're enlightened yet?") and brings it into direct dialogue with some objective, quantifiable markers increasingly verifiable in the emerging field of neuroscience. It allows us to look at the concept/experience of nonduality not through the lens of personal spiritual attainment but through the lens of the continuing evolution of consciousness.

According to this way of looking at things, the "lower" levels of consciousness (first and second tiers on Wilber's maps, up to and including the integral level) all work with increasingly sophisticated refinement of the classic binary hardwiring—"perception through differentiation." The brain sets up the perceptual field with an implicit "inside" and "outside" (with one's innermost sense of identity squarely at the center of the inside, holding down the post of "I"). The world swirling around outside is then navigated by breaking it up into finite bits (known as "descriptors," or individual characteristics), which are then manipulated through a set of standard binary operations—"more/less," "better/worse," "good/bad," and so on. In this operating system identity is conferred by what differentiates you from everything else, and to be "self-aware" means to be able to stand outside yourself and reflect back on yourself, or to be able to navigate your way forward or backward along the arrow of time through your memory and imagination. This is the fabled "self-reflexive consciousness," the mind that has brought the Western world into existence—the "I think, therefore I am" mind upon which the foundations of modern civilization rest. And it is, to be sure, a wonder, an extraordinary evolutionary breakthrough. But it is not all there is, nor is it even remotely the endpoint.

Imagine that there might be a different way of structuring the field of perception, an alternative way of wiring the brain that did not depend on that initial bifurcation of the perceptual field into inside and outside, subject and object. Instead, one would grasp the entire pattern as a whole—*holographically*—through a perceptual modality quantitatively more immediate and sensate, working on vibrational resonance rather than mental abstraction. Then one would indeed experience that signature sense of oneness—not, however, because one had broken into a whole new realm of spiritual experience, but because that tedious, "translator" mechanism of the self-reflective brain has finally been superseded. You see oneness because you see *from* oneness.

This would be my own working definition of nonduality.

From this quantum shift in the hardwiring of perception, of course, the much celebrated spiritual and moral attainments would understandably flow, since a mind that does not need to separate and exclude in order to perceive reality will encounter far less resistance in the current of life and inflict far less violence upon others. But they are the *fruits* of this transformation in consciousness, not the essence of it. The essence is the ability to receive and relate information along a whole new trajectory of neurological synapses. It is measurable. And it is incremental.

This final approach cuts through so much of the "apples to oranges" confusion that inevitably results when we try to align metaphysical systems with very different values and measuring rods. It allows us to focus on what's actually going on in the brain, how the connections are actually being made, whether that brain belongs to a Buddhist approaching sunyata or a Christian apprehending the mystical union of all things in Christ. It allows us to focus on the underlying patterns of attention, self-sense, and synchrony (as opposed to linearity) that are the real tip-offs to the presence of stable nondual perception.

In particular, I believe, it also gives us a more quantifiable way to begin to approach Christianity's core intuition that the shift to this "upgraded" operating system has something to do with "putting the mind in the heart." Directly or indirectly this will be the underlying theme of this second section of my book. It is an oft-repeated cliché, particularly in the Christian East. But we need to hear—*really hear*—what it is saying.

And a Couple of "Also-Rans"

As I bring this chapter to a close, I need to mention two things that nondual does *not* mean. Both of the following popular clichés represent serious misunderstandings.

To begin with, nondual does *not* mean renouncing the capacity for critical thinking. This was a popular notion back in the nineties, when the term was first hitting the "spiritual but not religious" sector in a big way. Any attempt to exercise the mind, to think or draw closely reasoned arguments, met with the rejoinder "That's dualistic!" (The companion cliché, of course, is *"He's* in his head, but *she's* in her heart!") This is boomeritis nondualism, for sure, where enlightenment is equated with the abdication of all intellectual responsibility.

It's not a question of suspending the head, but of anchoring and entraining it within a deeper ground. If you hear His Holiness the Dalai Lama speak, or peruse the works of some of the most powerful of our Western mystical thinkers (from Meister Eckhart to Jesus to Raimon Panikkar to Edith Stein), you will see that nondual perception can and does express itself through the best of our human cognitive faculties, provided they are grounded in something deeper than mere abstraction and intellectualism.

Second: nondual is not the same as philosophical monism. Monism is an ancient philosophical tradition, represented in its purest form in some branches of Hindu Vedanta. It stipulates, in essence, that all begins in the One and returns to the One, that the impression of complexity and differentiation is simply part of the illusion of this world. Now certainly it is possible for an attained nondual consciousness to ascribe to this philosophical position and to flourish within it. But the two are not synonymous. It is also possible to hold to a philosophical monism from a rigidly dualistic and authoritarian mode of consciousness. And equally, it is possible to look upon the world from a nondual vantage point and still affirm the reality of change, movement, and the structures in which the formless so marvelously drapes itself; one simply sees them from the perspective of oneness. There is no implicit need to reduce multiplicity to a primal unity in order to lay claim to nondual perception. Many schools of Advaita Vedanta suggest strongly that the Advaitic state is "not one, not two, but both one and two." And this is crucially important as we look at the mystical traditions of the West, for if we hold to the strict definition that nondual implies an adherence to the monist position, it will be a foregone conclusion that nothing in the Western tradition merits the title nondual.

And this would surely be to throw out the baby with the bathwater.

CHAPTER 2

The Way of the Heart

"Put the mind in the heart. . . . Put the mind in the heart. . . . Stand before the Lord with the mind in the heart." From page after page in the *Philokalia,* that hallowed collection of spiritual writings from the Christian East, this same refrain emerges. It is striking in both its insistence and its specificity. Whatever that exalted level of spiritual attainment is conceived to be— whether you call it "salvation," "enlightenment," "contemplation," or "divine union"—*this* is the inner configuration in which it is found. This and no other.

It leaves one wondering what these old spiritual masters actually *knew* and—if it's even remotely as precise and anatomically grounded as it sounds—why this knowledge has not factored more prominently in contemporary typologies of consciousness.

Part of the problem as this ancient teaching falls on contemporary ears is that we will inevitably be hearing it through a modern filter that does not serve it well. In our own times the word "heart" has come to be associated primarily with the emotions (as opposed to the mental operations of the mind), and so the instruction will be inevitably heard as "get out of your mind and into your emotions"—which is, alas, pretty close to 180 degrees from what the instruction is actually saying.

Yes, it is certainly true that the heart's native language is affectivity—perception through deep feelingness. But it may come as a shock to contemporary seekers to learn that the things we nowadays identify with the feeling life—passion, drama, intensity, compelling emotion—are qualities that in the ancient anatomical treatises were associated not with the heart but with the *liver*! They are signs of agitation and turbidity (an excess of bile!) rather than authentic feelingness. In fact, they are traditionally seen as the *roadblocks* to the authentic feeling life, the saboteurs that steal its energy and distort its true nature.

And so before we can even begin to unlock the wisdom of these ancient texts, we need to gently set aside our contemporary fascination with emotivity as the royal road to spiritual authenticity and return to the classic understanding from which these teachings emerge, which features the heart in a far more spacious and luminous role.

According to the great wisdom traditions of the West (Christian, Jewish, Islamic), the heart is first and foremost *an organ of spiritual perception*. Its primary function is to look beyond the obvious, the boundaried surface of things, and see into a deeper reality, emerging from some unknown profundity, which plays lightly upon the surface of this life without being caught there: a world where meaning, insight, and clarity come together in a whole different way. Saint Paul talked about this other kind of perceptivity with the term "faith" ("Faith is the substance of things hoped for, the evidence of things not seen"), but the word "faith" is itself often misunderstood by the linear mind. What it really designates is not a leaping into the dark (as so often misconstrued) but a subtle *seeing* in the dark, a kind of spiritual night vision that allows one to see with inner certainty that the elusive golden thread glimpsed from within actually does lead somewhere.

Perhaps the most comprehensive definition of this wider spiritual perceptivity is from Kabir Helminski, a modern Sufi master. I realize that I quote it in nearly every book I have written, but I do so because it is so fundamental to the wisdom tradition that I have come to know as the authentic heart of Christianity. Here it is yet again:

We have subtle subconscious faculties we are not using. Beyond the limited analytic intellect is a vast realm of mind that includes psychic and extrasensory abilities; intuition; wisdom; a sense of unity; aesthetic, qualitative and creative faculties; and image-forming and symbolic capacities. Though these faculties are many, we give them a single name with some justification for they are working best when they are in concert. They comprise a mind, moreover, in spontaneous connection to the cosmic mind. This total mind we call "heart."[1]

"The heart," Helminski continues,

is the antenna that receives the emanations of subtler levels of existence. The human heart has its proper field of function beyond the limits of the superficial, reactive ego-self. Awakening the heart, or the spiritualized mind, is an unlimited process of making the mind more sensitive, focused, energized, subtle, and refined, of joining it to its cosmic milieu, the infinity of love.[2]

Now it may concern some of you that you're hearing Islamic teaching here, not Christian. And it may well be true that this understanding of the heart as "spiritualized mind"— "the organ prepared by God for contemplation"[3]—has been brought to its subtlest and most comprehensive articulation in the great Islamic Sufi masters. As early as the tenth century, Al-Hakîm al Tirmidhî's masterful *Treatise on the Heart* laid the foundations for an elaborate Sufi understanding of the heart as a tripartite physical, emotional, and spiritual organ.[4] On this foundation would gradually rise an expansive repertory of spiritual practices supporting this increasingly "sensitive, focused, energized, subtle, and refined" heart attunement.

But it's right there in Christianity as well. Aside from the incomparable Orthodox teachings on Prayer of the Heart collected in the *Philokalia,* it's completely scriptural. Simply open your Bible to the Beatitudes (Matthew 5:8) and read the words straight from Jesus himself: "Blessed are the pure in heart, for they shall see God."

We will return to what "pure in heart" means in due course. But clearly Jesus had a foundational grasp on the heart as an organ of spiritual perception, and he had his own highly specific method for catalyzing this quantum leap in human consciousness. I have written extensively about this in my book *The Wisdom Jesus,* in which I lay out the principles of his kenotic ("letting go") spirituality as a pathway of conscious transformation leading to nondual awakening. You will see there how this goal formed the core of his teaching, hidden in plain sight for twenty centuries now. I will be drawing on this material from time to time as it becomes pertinent to our present exploration. For now, the essential point is simply to realize that the teaching on the heart is not intrinsically an "Islamic" revelation, any more than it is a "Christian" one. If anything, its headwaters lie in that great evolutionary incubator of Judaism, in which more and more in those final centuries before the Common Era, the great Israelite prophets begin to sense a new evolutionary star rising on the horizon of consciousness. Yahweh is about to do something new, about to up the ante in the continuing journey of mutual self-disclosure that has formed the basis of the covenant with Israel. The prophet Ezekiel gets it the most directly, as the following words of revelation tumble from his mouth, directly from the heart of God:

> I will take you from the nations and gather you from all the countries, and bring you into your own land. I will sprinkle clean water upon you, and you shall be clean from all your uncleannesses, and from all your idols I will cleanse you. A new heart I will give you, and a new spirit I will put within you; and I will remove from your body the heart of stone and give you a heart of flesh. I will put my spirit within you and make you follow my statutes and be careful to observe my ordinances. Then you shall live in the land I gave to your ancestors, and you shall be my people and I will be your God.
> *(Ezekiel 36:24–28)*

A new interiority is dawning on the horizon, a new capacity to read the pattern from within: to live the covenant without a need for external forms and regulations, simply by living it from an inner integrity. And for the first time in Western history, this capacity to see from within is explicitly linked to the heart, and specifically to a "heart of flesh."

Without any attempt to end-run the massive theological and historical parameters that have grown up around this issue, my bare-bones take on Jesus is that he comes as the "master cardiologist," the next in the great succession of Hebrew prophets, to do that "heart surgery" first announced by Ezekiel. And his powerfully original (at least in terms of anything heretofore seen in the Semitic lands) method of awakening heart perceptivity—through a radical nonclinging or "letting go"—will in fact reveal itself as the tie rod connecting everything I am talking about in this book.

Do I Really Mean the Physical Heart?

Not to be naive here, but yes. We are indeed talking about the physical heart, at least insofar as it furnishes our bodily anchor for all those wondrous voyages into far-flung spiritual realms.

Again, the Eastern Orthodox tradition is not in the least equivocal on this point. Lest there be any tendency to hear the word as merely symbolic of some "innermost essence" of a person, the texts direct us immediately to the chest, where the sign that prayer is progressing will be a palpable physical warmth:

> To stand guard over the heart, to stand with the mind in the heart, to descend from the head to the heart—all these are one and the same thing. The core of the work lies in concentrating the attention and the standing before the invisible Lord, not in the head but in the chest, close to the heart and in the heart. When the divine warmth comes, all this will be clear.[5]

The following instruction is even more specific:

> When we read in the writings of the Fathers about the place of the heart which the mind finds by way of prayer, we must understand by this the spiritual faculty that exists in the heart. Placed by the creator in the upper part of the heart, this spiritual faculty distinguishes the human heart from the heart of animals . . . The intellectual faculty in man's soul, though spiritual, dwells in the brain, that is to say in the head: in the same way, the spiritual faculty which we term the spirit of man, though spiritual, dwells in the upper part of the heart, close to the left nipple of the chest and a little above it.[6]

While the sheer physicality of this may make some readers squirm, the contemporary phenomenologist Robert Sardello is another strong advocate for a full inclusion of the physical heart in any serious consideration of the spirituality of the heart. When he speaks of the heart, as he makes clear in his remarkable book *Silence: The Mystery of Wholeness,* he is always referring to "the physical organ of the heart," which merits this special consideration precisely because "it functions simultaneously as a physical, psychic, and spiritual organ."[7] It is this seamlessly tripartite nature of the heart's field of activity that bestows its unusual transformative powers. While there are many spiritual traditions that focus on "the heart as the instrument through which religious practices take place," Sardello feels that "these traditions do not focus on the inherent activity of the heart, which is already an act of a spiritual nature."[8]

To demonstrate what this "inherently spiritual nature" of the heart might feel like, Sardello leads his readers on a profound voyage of discovery into the inner chambers of their own heart. Wielding those two classic tools of inner work, attention and sensation, he teaches us how to access the heart through concentrated sensation (rather than visualization or emotion) and there discover its inherent vibrational signature as "pure intimacy . . . intimacy without something or someone attached to that intimacy."[9]

I have to say I followed that exercise several times and was astonished by the results. I had experienced something of that "pure intimacy" before, as that sort of golden tenderness that sometimes surrounds a period of Centering Prayer. But never had I experienced it with such force or clarity, as a distinct inner bandwidth resonating in perfect synchrony with (in Kabir Helminski's words) "its cosmic milieu, the infinity of love." No wonder the embodied aspect of heart spirituality is so important! For it is only through sensation—that is, "attention concentrated in the heart"—that this experience of utter fullness and belonging becomes accessible.[10]

Sardello is not the only voice in the field. There is now a substantial and growing body of "bridge literature" linking classic spiritual teachings on the heart with emerging discoveries in the field of neurobiology. I have already mentioned the pioneering work of the HeartMath Institute, but I want to call attention to two other fascinating and useful books for the spiritually adventurous nonspecialist: *The Biology of Transcendence* by Joseph Chilton Pearce[11] and *The Secret Teaching of Plants* by Stephen Harrod Buhner.[12] Marshaling considerable scientific data in a format easily accessible to a lay reader, each of these books demonstrates how contemporary science has taken us far beyond the notion of the heart as a mechanical pump to revision it as "an electromagnetic generator,"[13] working simultaneously across a range of vibrational frequencies to perform its various tasks of internal and external self-regulation and information exchange. (An "organ of spiritual perception," after all, can be understood in this context as simply an electromagnetic generator picking up information at far subtler vibrational bandwidths.) Both books call attention, as does the HeartMath Institute, to the intricate feedback loops between heart and brain—almost as if the human being were expressly wired to facilitate this exchange, which Pearce sees as fundamentally between the universal (carried in the heart) and the particular (carried in the brain). As he expresses it, "The heart takes on the subtle individual colors of a person without losing its essential universality. It seems to mediate between our individual self and a universal process while being representative of that universal process."[14] While such bold statements may make hard-core scientists writhe, from the spiritual side of the bridge it is easily comprehensible and brings additional confirmation that "putting the mind in the heart" is not merely a quaint spiritual metaphor but contains precise and essential information on the physiological under-girding of conscious transformation.

What Gets in the Way?

According to Western understanding, the heart does not need to be "grown" or "evolved." Every heart is already a perfect holograph of the divine heart, carrying within itself full access to the information of the whole. But it does need to be *purified*, as Jesus himself observed. In its spiritual capacity, the heart is fundamentally a homing beacon, allowing us to stay aligned with those "emanations from more subtle levels of existence" Helminski refers to, and hence to follow the authentic path of our own unfolding. But when the signals get jammed by the interference of lower-level noise, then it is no longer able to do its beaconing work.

Unanimously, the Christian wisdom tradition proclaims that the source of this lower-level noise is "the passions." As the *Philokalia* repeatedly emphasizes, the problem with the passions is that *they divide the heart*.[15] A heart that is divided, pulled this way and that by competing inner agendas, is like a wind-tossed sea: unable to reflect on its surface the clear image of the moon.

Here again is a teaching that tends to set contemporary people's teeth on edge. I know this from personal experience, because the issue comes up at nearly every workshop I give. To our modern Western way of hearing, "passion" is a good thing: something akin to élan vital, the source of our aliveness and motivation. It is to be encouraged, not discouraged. At a recent workshop I led, a bishop approached me with some concern and explained that in his diocese, following the recommendations of a church consultant, he had managed to boost morale and productivity by significant percentages simply by encouraging his clergy "to follow their passions."

Well-nigh universally today, the notion of "passionlessness" (a quality eagerly sought after in the ancient teachings of the desert fathers and mothers) equates to "emotionally brain dead." If you take away passion, what is left?

So once again we have to begin with some decoding.

If you consult any English dictionary, you will discover that the word "passion" comes from the Latin verb *patior*, which means "to suffer" (*passio* is the first-person singular). But this still doesn't get us all the way, because the literal, now largely archaic, meaning of the verb "to suffer" (to "undergo or experience") is literally *to be acted upon*. The chief operative here is the involuntary and mechanical aspect of the transaction. And according to the traditional wisdom teachings, it is precisely that involuntary and mechanical aspect of being "grabbed" that leads to suffering in the sense of how we use the term today. Thus, in the ancient insights on which this spiritual teaching rests, passion did not mean élan vital, energy, or aliveness. It designated being stuck, grabbed, and blindly reactive.

This original meaning is clearly uppermost in the powerful teaching of the fourth-century desert father Evagrius Ponticus. Sometimes credited with being the first spiritual psychologist in the Christian West, Evagrius developed a marvelously subtle teaching on the progressive nature of emotional entanglement, a teaching that would eventually bear fruit in the fully articulated doctrine of the seven deadly sins. His core realization was that when the first stirrings of what will eventually become full-fledged passionate outbursts appear on the screen of consciousness, they begin as "thoughts"—*logismoi*, in his words—streams of associative logic following well-conditioned inner tracks. At first they are merely that—"thought-loops," mere flotsam on the endlessly moving river of the mind. But at some point a thought-loop will entrain with one's sense of identity—an emotional value or point of view is suddenly at stake—and then one is hooked. A passion is born, and the emotions spew forth. Thomas Keating has marvelously re-packaged this ancient teaching in his diagram of the life cycle of an emotion,[16] a core part of his Centering Prayer teaching. This diagram makes clear that once the emotion is engaged, once that sense of "I" locks in, what follows is a full-scale emotional uproar—which then, as Father Keating points out, simply drives the syndrome deeper and deeper into the unconscious, where it becomes even more involuntary and mechanically triggered.

What breaks the syndrome? For Evagrius, liberation lies in *an increasingly developed inner capacity to notice when a thought is beginning to take on emotional coloration and to nip it in the bud before it becomes a passion by dis-identifying or disengaging from it.* This is the essence of the teaching that has held sway in our tradition for more than a thousand years.

Now, of course, there are various ways of going about this disengaging. Contemporary psychology has added the important qualifier that disengaging is not the same thing as *repressing* (which is simply sweeping the issue under the psychological rug) and has developed important methodologies for allowing people to become consciously present to and "own" the stew fermenting within them. But it must also be stated that "owning" does not automatically entail either "acting out" or verbally "expressing" that emotional uproar. Rather, the genius of the earlier tradition has been to insist that if one can merely back the identification out—that sense of "me," stuck to a fixed frame of reference or value—then the energy being co-opted and squandered in useless emotional turmoil can be recaptured at a higher level to strengthen the intensity and clarity of heart perceptivity. Rather than fueling the "reactive ego-self," the energy can be "rejoined to its cosmic milieu, the infinity of love." And that, essentially, constitutes the goal of purification—at least as it has been understood in service of conscious transformation.

Emotion versus Feeling

Here again, we have an important clarification contributed by Robert Sardello. Echoing the classic understanding of the Christian Inner tradition (I first encountered this teaching in the Gurdjieff Work), Sardello points out that most of us use the terms "feeling" and "emotion" interchangeably, as if they are synonyms. They are not. Emotion is technically "stuck" feeling, feeling bound to a fixed point of view or fixed reference point. "We are not free in our emotional life," he points out, since emotion always "occurs quite automatically as a reaction to something that happens to us."[17] It would correspond to what Helminski calls "the heart in service to the reactive ego-self."

Beyond this limited sphere opens up a vast reservoir of feelingness. Here the currents run hard and strong, always tinged with a kind of multivalence in which the hard-and-fast boundaries distinguishing one emotion from another begin to blend together. Happiness is tinged with sadness, grief touches at its bottomless depths the mysterious upwelling of comfort, loneliness is suffused with intimacy, and the deep ache of yearning for the absent beloved becomes the paradoxical sacrament of presence. "For beauty is only the beginning of a terror we can just scarcely bear," observes Rilke, "and the reason we adore it so is that it serenely disdains to destroy us."[18]

Such is the sensation of the heart beginning to swim in those deeper waters, awakening to its birthright as an organ of spiritual perception. And it would stand to reason, of course, that the experience is feeling-ful because that is the heart's modus operandi; it gains information by entering the inside of things and coming into resonance with them. But this is feeling of an entirely different order, no longer affixed to a personal self-center, but flowing in holographic union with that which can always and only flow, the great dynamism of love. "Feeling as a form of knowing"[19] becomes the pathway of this other mode of perceptivity, more intense, but strangely familiar and effortless.

The great wager around which the Western Inner tradition has encamped is that as one is able to release the heart from its enslavement to the passions, this other heart emerges: this "organ of contemplation," of luminous sight and compassionate action. For what one "sees" and entrains with is none other than this higher order of divine coherence and compassion, which can be verified as objectively *real,* but becomes accessible only when the heart is able to rise to this highest level and assume its cosmically appointed function. Then grace upon grace flows through this vibrating reed and on out into a transfigured world: transfigured by the very grace of being bathed in this undivided light.

"Blessed are the pure in heart, for they shall see God." In this one sentence, the whole of the teaching is conveyed. What remains is for us to come to a greater understanding of how this purification is actually accomplished: a critical issue on which Christian tradition is by no means unanimous. This will be the subject of our next chapter.

CHAPTER 3

Centering Prayer and Attention of the Heart

In the thirty years now since Centering Prayer first moved beyond the walls of Saint Joseph's Abbey in Massachusetts to become a lay groundswell, it has certainly implanted itself deeply and (one hopes) permanently in the canon of Christian contemplative practice. Yet it still jostles somewhat uneasily against the walls of received tradition. I am not speaking here of fundamentalist-generated fear ("The devil will get you if you make your mind a blank"), but rather, of serious reservations on the part of some deeply formed in the Christian contemplative tradition that this prayer is somehow "breaking the rules." In its classic presentations, Christian prayer is "progressive"; it passes through stages. And the contemplative stage is traditionally regarded as the highest, or subtlest. "One does not take the kingdom by force," in the concluding words of a recent, thoughtful article by a well-prepared commentator.[1] Contemplation is approached by a gradual path leading from purgative to illuminative to unitive: from cataphatic to apophatic. The "ladder" of spiritual ascent is so deeply engrained on the Christian religious imagination that it seems virtually impossible to conceive of the journey in any other way. Contemplative prayer is "higher," and it is

approached only gradually through a long journey of purification and inner preparation.

But is this in fact really so?

"You have to experience duality for a long time until you
see it's not there," said Thomas Merton at a conference given
to the nuns of Redwoods Monastery shortly before boarding
the plane to Asia on the last leg of his human journey. "Don't
consider dualistic prayer on a lower level. The lower is higher.
There are no levels. At any moment you can break through
to the underlying unity which is God's gift in Christ. In the
end, Praise praises. Thanksgiving gives thanks. Jesus prays.
Openness is all."[2]

Certainly these words of unitive, realized mastery make it
clear that Merton "got there." But how? Was this breakthrough
insight the result of his long tread up the traditional ladder of
ascent—in other words, is he "exhibit A" of the assertion that
the classic monastic model works? Or is his unitive awakening
something more akin to Dorothy in the final scene of *The
Wizard of Oz,* when she realizes that all along the shoes that
would carry her home have been right there on her feet?

This is of course an impossible question to answer, and I do
not intend to do so directly, only to use it as a kind of leverage.
As the Mad Hatter so wisely quipped, "How you get there is
where you arrive," and Merton's journey could only have been
Merton's. And yet the door, once he found it, can only be seen
as the timeless and universal gate. Like a few others before him
and a few significant monastic others following in his wake
(Thomas Keating most prominently), he simply, in my estimate,
came upon that hidden "back door" or "wormhole" within
the Christian path that transports one out of the "progressive"
journey in linear time into the instantaneous, seamless fullness
from which prayer is always emerging.

And he found it in the same way that all who find it do so:
in the gathering awareness that the cave of the heart is entered

not only or even primarily through purification and concentration, but through surrender and release. This is the hidden, backdoor path that we will be exploring in this chapter. It has always been there as an alternative within Christian spiritual tradition to that "ladder of ascent": perhaps not as well known, but fully orthodox and in the end even more reliable, since it derives, ultimately, from the direct teaching and self-understanding of Jesus himself. It is from this alternative pathway that Centering Prayer derives its legitimacy and its powerful capacity to heal and unify.

Centering Prayer as
Self-Emptying Love

As part one of this book hopefully made clear, the method of Centering Prayer is founded entirely on the gesture of surrender, or letting go. Its theological foundation rests on the principle of kenosis (Philippians 2:6), Jesus's self-emptying love that forms the core of his own self-understanding and life practice. During the prayer time itself, surrender is practiced through the letting go of thoughts as they arise. Unlike other forms of meditation, neither a focused awareness nor a steady witnessing presence is required. There is no need to "follow" the thoughts as they arise, merely to promptly let them go as soon as one realizes one is engaged in thinking.

With committed practice, this well-rehearsed gesture of release is inwardly imprinted and begins to coalesce as a distinct "magnetic center" within you; it can actually be experienced on a subtle physical level as a "drop and release" in the solar plexus region of the body and as a tug to center. Of its own accord it begins to hold you at that place of deeper spiritual attentiveness during prayer time. Not long after this initial "tethering of the heart" has set in, most experienced practitioners begin to feel the tug even outside their times of prayer, in the midst of their daily rounds, reminding them of the deepening river of prayer that has begun to flow in them beneath the surface of their ordinary lives. The intent of Centering Prayer is not to "access" God through contemplative stillness or mystical experience, but to teach its practitioners how to spontaneously align with Jesus's own continuously creative and enfolding presence through emulating his kenotic practice in all life situations.

Thus the real measure of this prayer is not found during the prayer time itself; Centering Prayer neither seeks nor accepts[3] what is commonly known as "mystical experience." Instead, it is found in the gradual but steady capacity to conform a person to "the mind of Christ," and the life attitudes of compassion, generosity, and freedom that flow from this gesture.

"God should be with you like a toothache!" proclaimed the nineteenth-century Orthodox master Theophan the Recluse.[4] And while most of us might have preferred a gentler metaphor, it does speak forcefully to the fact that our concept of God is *sensate*. Remembrance of God is not a mental concept; it exists deeply embodied as a vibration, a homing frequency to which we can become increasingly sensitively attuned.

This growing experiential awareness of a magnetic center is very important, not only for your personal spiritual development but because of the new light it sheds on the ancient and venerable desideratum of the Western spiritual path: the goal of "putting the mind in the heart." As I hope to show here, it is against this backdrop that Centering Prayer's powerful and innovative contribution to the received wisdom of Western spirituality becomes fully apparent.

Surmounting Love by Love

As I observed in the preceding chapter, for most Western Christians the heart would more readily be associated with the capacity to *feel*. Its genius is emotional empathy. Even that old pop psychology cliché "being in the heart" versus "being in the head" rests on our staunch conviction that the heart mirrors the real person through its capacity to feel, to love, to empathize. If it has a capacity for spiritual perception, it is exercised through love. Hence the immortal instructions in *The Cloud of Unknowing:* "God may be reached and held close by means of love, but by means of thought never."[5]

It is not surprising, then, that overwhelmingly in the Western tradition, the core methodology for "putting the mind in the heart" can be described as *the concentration of affectivity.* In both the Christian East and the Christian West, the basic strategy for spiritual transformation begins by engaging the heart's natural capacity to feel. Once the heart has been stirred by strong emotions, it is a surprisingly short step to concentrate and purify these emotions through spiritual practice and harness their vibrant energy for spiritual awakening.

You can see the strategy already at work in the teachings of the fifth-century spiritual master John Cassian, particularly in his tenth conference, where he urges the continuous use of the prayer sentence from Psalm 70, "O Lord, come to my assistance, O God make speed to save me." Cassian goes on to explain: "It is not without good reason that this verse has been chosen from the whole of scripture as a device. For it contains within it all the feelings of which human nature is capable."[6] By embracing the full intensity of these feelings, an ardor is generated that catapults the heart free and clear of its egocentric orbit and straight into the heart of God.

In fact, as Christian contemplative masters have consistently observed from the desert times right down into our own, without that critical intensity of ardor, it is all but impossible to escape the centrifugal force of human egotism. It takes gold to make gold; a heart that burns, even with carnal love, can be directed toward contemplation of higher things, but a heart of stone travels nowhere. As Saint John Climacus observed with keen insight:

> I have seen impure souls who threw themselves headlong into physical *eros* to a frenzied degree. It was their very experience of that *eros* that led them to interior conversion. They concentrated their *eros* on the Lord. Rising above fear, they tried to love God with insatiable desire. That is why when Christ spoke to the woman who had been a sinner he did not say that she had been afraid, but that she had loved much, and had easily been able to surmount love by love.[7]

This goal of "surmounting love by love," or in other words, uniting the devotional and perceptive aspects of the heart in a single mystical flame, reveals the secret of why Christianity has always embraced affectivity as the gateway to inner awakening. We see this same predilection at work in the spiritual practice of *lectio divina*, where the third stage, *oratio*, is intended to take the concentrated attention of a mind that has gathered itself through *meditatio* and fan it to a level of emotional intensity wherein the boundaries of egoic consciousness are essentially melted, at least for the duration of the prayer. We see it again in the Jesus Prayer—"Lord Jesus Christ, have mercy on me,"—that foundational prayer of Orthodox spirituality. While superficially resembling a mantra, it in fact gains its force through the concentration of affective love.

This is also the underlying reason, I believe, that Christian tradition has never taken easily to meditation, and has never rested entirely comfortably with a methodology that seems to go against the grain of one of its most basic presuppositions: that it is not possible to reach the apophatic without first going through the cataphatic—that is, via the concentration of affectivity. Working with eros as its transformational quicksilver, the journey necessarily entails a long, tough slog through the gristmills of purification and inner preparation before the soul is ready to "bear the beams of love" (in the words of William Blake) in pure contemplation. By an overwhelming majority, the pedagogy of both the Christian West and the Christian East has favored this developmental trajectory.

Attention of the Heart

But majority is not the same thing as exclusive. While "concentration of affectivity" clearly dominates the field in Christian spirituality, there is also a different pathway to center, and one who was onto it was Simeon the New Theologian. His curiously little-known essay "Three Methods of Attention and Prayer" is one of the most important resources available for locating Centering Prayer within the wider tradition of Christian interior prayer and for validating its innovative yet entirely orthodox starting points.[8]

I have already spoken of Simeon extensively in my book *Centering Prayer and Inner Awakening,* but let me briefly recap some of the essential points. Simeon was one of the most brilliant spiritual theologians of his day, or of any day. His life span (949–1022) places him almost exactly a thousand years ago, but the issues he was grappling with in the eleventh century are still cutting-edge in our own times. Essentially, Simeon insisted on the dimension of *conscious presence* in our human relationship with the divine—or as he called it, "attention of the heart."

Developing this kind of attention is all-important, Simeon maintains, for otherwise, "It is impossible to have purity of heart; impossible to fulfill the Beatitudes."[9] Only when the mind is "in the heart," grounded and tethered in that deeper wellspring of spiritual awareness, is it possible to live the teachings of Jesus without hypocrisy or burnout. The gospel requires a radical openness and compassion that is beyond the capacity of the anxious, fear-ridden ego.

But how to swim down to these deeper waters? Simeon lays out three possibilities. The first is the classic path of "concentration of affectivity" as we have just described it:

> If a man stands at prayer and, raising his hands, his eyes and his mind to heaven, keeps in mind Divine thoughts, imagines celestial blessings, hierarchies of angels and dwellings of the saints, assembles briefly in his mind all he has learnt from the Holy Scriptures and ponders over all this while at prayer, gazing up to heaven, and thus inciting his soul to longing and love of God, at times even shedding tears and weeping, this will be the first method of attention and prayer.[10]

The problem with this traditional method, Simeon asserts, is that it relies on a high level of excitement of the external faculties, which is ultimately self-delusional and can become addictive, leading one to depend on lights, sweet scents, and "other like phenomena" as evidence of the presence of God. "If then such a man give himself up to silence," Simeon adds bluntly, "he can scarcely avoid going out of his mind."[11]

The second method he explores is self-examination and the collecting of thoughts "so that they cease to wander"—the classic methodology of a practice based on awareness. This approach relies heavily on the practices of inner attention, self-remembering, and the examination of consciousness. But the fatal flaw in this methodology, Simeon observes, is that such a practitioner "remains in the head, whereas evil thoughts are generated in the heart."[12] In other words, the aspiring seeker is likely to be blindsided by the strength of his or her unconscious impulses.

Simeon designates the third method as *attention of the heart* and describes it as follows:

> You should observe three things before all else: freedom from all cares, not only cares about bad and vain but even about good things ... Your conscience should be clear so that it denounces you in nothing, and you should have a complete absence of passionate attachment, so that your thought inclines to nothing worldly.[13]

The importance of Simeon's observation here is extraordinary, for he has essentially described the practice of kenotic surrender. That greatest desideratum of the spiritual life, attention of the heart, is achieved, he feels, not so much by concentration of affectivity as by the simple release of all that one is clinging to, the good things as well as the bad things. He proposes that we start with that bare gesture of letting go. Attention of the heart can certainly be engaged through concentrated affectivity. But it can also, just as well, be engaged through relinquishing the passions and relaxing the will.

While Simeon is clearly describing an integrated practice combining both prayer and daily life, it is uncanny how closely his words dovetail with the basic methodology of Centering Prayer. As a person sits in Centering Prayer attempting to "resist no thought, retain no thought, react to no thought," he or she is actually progressing in small but utterly real increments toward "freedom from all cares" and "the absence of passionate attachments." This is Simeon's "attention of the heart," which he states is inseparable from true prayer and true conversion. In fact, the case can be made that what Thomas Keating has really succeeded in doing is to give meditational form to Simeon's attention of the heart, thereby providing a powerful new access point to the traditional wisdom of the Christian inner path. His approach, like Simeon's, is innovative but entirely orthodox once you understand where he is coming from. The tie-in between Centering Prayer and Simeon's attention of the heart is simply another link in the chain situating Centering Prayer firmly within the lineage of Christian kenosis understood as spiritual path.

Finding the Way to the Heart

"Keep your mind there [in the heart]," remarks Simeon, "trying by every possible means to find the place where the heart is." In his *Lost Christianity,* Jacob Needleman immediately picks up on the irony of this: that as we begin, we do not know where the heart is. We must learn, through the process of repeated tuning in.[14]

My hunch is that this describes the actual journey of both Thomas Merton and Thomas Keating—and undoubtedly Simeon as well. During their respective monastic novitiates, "the first method of attention and prayer" was what was available, and they each practiced it to its fullness. (And even in the early days of Centering Prayer teaching, the sacred word was initially described as a "love word": affectivity in capsule form, or in other words, an intense, concentrated version of "all those feelings known to man."[15]) It was ultimately through the experience of contemplation itself that these spiritual masters came to their realization that all along it has been the surrender carrying them home.

In his inimitable way, Merton puts words to the bare-bones truth of this timeless moment: the "aha" realization that solves Simeon's (and Needleman's) koan of "the way to the heart":

This act of total surrender is not merely a fantastic intellectual and mystical gamble; it is something much more serious: it is an act of love for this unseen Person Who, in the very gift of love by which we surrender ourselves to His reality, also makes His presence known to us.[16]

If what he glimpses in this remarkable insight is true, then the response to those overly concerned that Centering Prayer is violating the traditional pedagogy can only be a gentle "All shall be well, and all manner of things shall be well." For ultimately, as this "unseen person" becomes present, the knee of the heart will instinctively bow—and the rest will somehow work itself out.

It is indeed true that ego-driven spiritual ambitiousness can wind up in very bad places. But it is important never to lose sight of the fact that *spiritual ambitiousness and attention of the heart are mutually exclusive categories.* The proud may fall, but it will not be through following the way of the heart, for the heart has its inbuilt safeguard: it perceives only in the modality of surrender (which means, literally, to "hand oneself over," to entrust oneself entirely). In other words, the heart can fulfill its function as organ of spiritual perception only to the degree that it is able to bring itself into moral alignment with "the infinity of love" (in Kabir Helminski's words): to the extent that it is willing and able to coincide with love, to become love itself. For love is the ultimate, and ultimately the *only,* purification. But this "Love which moves the sun and the stars" is not a feeling, an eros fixated upon God; it is rather the alchemical agape that comes into being when eros becomes whole in the act of giving itself away. Whenever and wherever along the pathway of prayer this great secret is learned, it instantaneously reorganizes the playing field.

CHAPTER 4

Centering Prayer as Witnessing Practice

Why is this so difficult? In the decade since my *Centering Prayer and Inner Awakening* first made its appearance, I can say without hesitation that the topic that has generated the most puzzlement—in fact, downright unease—has been my chapter on the "inner observer." For some reason this concept does not come easily to Christians, nor sit comfortably within familiar reference points. Shortly before his death, Father Basil Pennington (the third monk in that Trappist triumvirate who brought the world Centering Prayer) had penned a highly critical review of that chapter, decrying it as "esoteric" and "non-Christian." Another monk in the community persuaded him to withdraw the review, but Thomas Keating himself has wondered to me whether this topic is "too advanced for most Centering Prayer practitioners."

I had to smile when he made this comment, during a conversation a couple of years ago. "Well, Fr. Thomas, if Oprah Winfrey and millions of others around the planet are learning the practice from Eckhart Tolle, it can't be *that* advanced." But the unease about its place in Christian contemplative tradition continues.

Part of the problem is that most of the prominent Christian spiritual teachers today, when they hear the term, set the bar either too low or too high. For Gerald May, cofounder of the influential Shalem Institute for Spiritual Formation, the observer (or witnessing presence) was always identified with "self-image": the egoic superego self-consciously meddling in the natural flow of awareness. May saw it as an artificial and usually judgmental imposter, splitting of the field of consciousness into subject and object, do and don't, should and should not. And for sure, this egoic meddler is well known in the various schools of inner witnessing; it is usually called "the egoic spectatator."[1] But this pesky pretender is a far cry from the true inner observer, and getting beyond it is simply a step on the learning curve.

The other misunderstanding is to set the bar too high, as Thomas Keating does—largely, I believe, under the influence of contemporary philosopher Ken Wilber. According to Wilber's basically Eastern road maps, witnessing is "a very high state" (as Keating has reported it to me), associated with the nameless and ever-present selfhood that retains consciousness even in dreamless sleep.[2] To be sure, this stable Witness (with a capital W) is indeed the subtlest realization of the gamut of witnessing. But witnessing *is* a gamut, and between those two extremities of egoic spectator and attained Witness unfolds a whole continuum of spiritual experience. When rightly understood and undertaken, the practice of inner observing does in fact unfold an interior pathway from the nervous, meddling ego to a more spacious and unboundaried consciousness fully at home in the infinite.

Thomas Keating fully recognizes the witnessing *function,* of course, even though he does not identify it by that name. When he speaks in one of his *Spiritual Journey* videos[3] about how contemplative practice allows a person to view life's inevitable emotional upsets like "a second-rate movie"—"You realize you can just walk out!"—he is describing precisely the ordinary domain of witnessing practice. Whatever it is that allows us to take a step back from the vicious circle of reactions, commentaries, and attractions/aversions that keep us glued to false self "programs for happiness" in fact unfolds within the sphere of witnessing. Functionally, Keating's metaphor of walking out of the movie covers exactly the same territory that Eckhart Tolle describes as the emergence from "ordinary unconsciousness" into "awareness of being": "What I call ordinary unconsciousness means being identified with your thought processes and emotions, your reactions, desires, and aversions. It is most people's normal state. In that state you are run by the egoic mind, and you are unaware of Being."[4]

"Awareness of Being" is what witnessing is fundamentally all about. And whether this Being is experienced as an "it," a "who," or a more indescribable sense of inner positioning (we will be looking more closely at this shortly), most the great spiritual paths insist that without some fluency in inner observation, we will never move beyond the egoic, narrative self with its endless stories that most of us mistake for the seat of our personal selfhood. In fact, "the unobserved mind" is Tolle's succinct definition for egoic selfhood itself.

Not Who, but What . . .

Who is this inner witness? Unfortunately, that is the wrong question to ask. It reifies witnessing into a "person" cohabiting your consciousness and sends you off on a wild goose chase to determine the identity of this hypothetical person. In various traditions the witness has been identified with "Real I," "the true self," and "essential being," but all of this naming misses the point. Witnessing is, if anything, a *verb*: an innate capacity of human consciousness to be present to itself as a field of awareness. Though personal, it is not a person—not an *other*—but a subtle capacity of consciousness itself, so far as we know gifted to the human species alone. Its purpose seems to be to keep track simultaneously of the horizontal axis—our life in time—and the pure divine awareness that is always intersecting this axis. Robert Sardello refers to it as "encompassing consciousness,"[5] and that is as good a job description as any. It is a more spacious way of being within oneself, of not losing the forest for the trees. Some would even say that this conscious interweaving of the horizontal and vertical (or finite and infinite) dimensions of existence is the specific cosmic task we humans are charged with, as our part in the mysterious alchemy of divine self-manifestation.

Basil Pennington's reservations notwithstanding, the idea of witnessing is authentically represented Christian tradition. In this chapter I will be drawing on a number of voices from both the Western and Orthodox contemplative streams who demonstrate both a clear recognition of the practice itself and a mature grasp of its subtleties. One of the most powerful descriptions of the witnessing state, in fact, comes from the same medieval Carthusian monk who gave us *The Cloud of Unknowing,* the primary source for Centering Prayer. In a later work, traditionally known as *The Book of Privy Counsel,* this anonymous monk describes what he calls a "dark contemplation of the substance of one's being" in ways that precisely match Ken Wilber's description of the attained state of Witnessing presence:

> For in this dark contemplation of the substance of your being, in which, I have told you, you are one with God, you must do all that you have to do: eat and drink, sleep and awaken, walk and sit, speak and be silent, lie down and get up, stand and kneel, run and ride, labor and rest. Every day you must offer it up to God as the most

precious offering you can make. It must take the first place of all your activity, whether what you are doing be styled active or contemplative.[6]

Doubled Attention or Unified Field?

But how do we learn to do this? To be sure, this is the fundamental challenge in witnessing practice. It seems as though we are being asked to hold some of our attention *in reserve* (in order to engage in that "dark contemplation") while we simultaneously go about our daily affairs. But how?

The classic strategy set forth by schools of inner work is to make use of the mind's capacity for "doubled attention": the capacity to split the field of attention and concentrate on two things simultaneously. As we "eat and drink, sleep and awaken," we are also reserving some part of our attention to "remember ourselves" (as the witnessing state is known in the Gurdjieff Work, where I did my own inner training). We practiced this doubled attention assiduously during my ten years of involvement in this Work.[7]

But it is precisely this instruction that many people find so awkward and frustrating. For Gerald May and his colleague Tilden Edwards, "remembrance of being" sounds like "*reflecting* on being," interposing a cumbersome and patently artificial intermediary between being and its direct perception, like a rock in the stream of consciousness.[8] If the error gets compounded by asking the question, "*Who* is the one who observes?" the result can be a spiraling hall of mirrors as the observer observes the observer observing the observer—right on into temporary schizophrenia! The whole project is simply too mental, one part of the mind spying on another.

The tenth-century Orthodox spiritual master Simeon the New Theologian, whom we met already in the last chapter, acutely spotted another difficulty with this traditional strategy of inner observation. Although the word "dissociation" had not yet been invented, he was keenly aware of the self-delusion that can all too easily result when an overly mental witnessing presence thinks it is keeping watch on itself but is in fact blindsided by its unconscious impulses. In his previously introduced "Three Methods of Attention and Prayer," recall how Simeon describes with meticulous irony the laborious and stylized operations of the cerebral "Witness" at its work of doubled attention:

> The second method [of prayer] is this: a man tears his mind away from all sensed objects and leads it within himself, guarding his senses and collecting his thoughts, so that they cease to wander . . . now with great labour and self-exertion strives to come back to himself after being caught and vanquished by some passion.[9]

"The distinctive feature of this method," Simeon recognizes, however, "is that it takes place in the head, thought fighting against thought." And the danger is all too obvious:

> In this struggle against himself a man can never be at peace in himself . . . Such a man is like one fighting his enemies in the dark . . . because he remains in the head, whereas evil thoughts are generated in the heart. He does not even see them, for his attention is not in his heart.[10]

In this passage, our attention may be momentarily co-opted by Simeon's striking statement that "evil thoughts are generated in the heart." Remember that Jesus himself made an identical assertion in Matthew 15:17 ("It is from the heart that evil deeds come: murder, adultery, immorality, theft, lies, slander"). The initial shock that this teaching produces on

modern ears can be somewhat softened by the recognition that
for an era in which the notion of the unconscious had not yet
been invented, the heart was seen as the seat of all motivation
not directly under conscious control, including what we would
nowadays call both the personal and transpersonal aspects.
In this context, then, Simeon's observation is in basically the
same ballpark as Thomas Keating's familiar contemporary
teaching, "The false self does not drop dead on request."

But if you push on and read Simeon's comment very alertly,
there in his last sentence you will notice a subtle nuance that
in effect offers the resolution to the dilemma we have been
pondering. Of this failed spiritual practitioner, Simeon does
not say "his attention is not *on* his heart," but rather "his
attention is not *in* his heart." And on that tiny preposition, I
believe, turns the whole key to the riddle of inner witnessing.

It is hard to think of attention as anything other than "on."
We almost cannot speak the words "pay attention" without adding the "*to*," so strong is the pull of this mysterious
energy field to establish itself in a subject/object relationship.
Traditional concentrative meditation methods know this well
and give the mind a simple object to focus its attention on:
breathing, a mantra, an icon.[11]

But attention is not only a carbon arc shooting from
subject to object. It is also an energy field in its own right—a
subtle *substance,* some schools of inner work teach, of extremely fine vibration. And while the subject/object modality
is its usual configuration, it can also be held inwardly and
experienced as a vibrational field in its own right: a coiled
latency, "quivering" (in the words of the poet Rumi) "like a
drop of mercury."[12] In this configuration, it does not "reflect
on being," but rather, directly *reflects* it: mirrors it like a still
pond, shimmering with the same vibrant "I am" presence. It
becomes a small, intensely concentrated reservoir of being
within oneself, a fountain of "spondic" energy (as Beatrice

Bruteau calls it; see ahead, p. 87) that does not need to be paid attention to, because it itself is the *subject* of attention, not the object. When one begins to get the knack of that experience, a sudden shift of direction occurs within, as one becomes viscerally aware of the difference between keeping one's attention "on" and keeping it "in."

In her masterful essay "Prayer and Identity," the contemporary nondual philosopher Beatrice Bruteau expands brilliantly on this slight but telling difference. After her opening assertion that "the work of prayer is to transform our sense of identity,"[13] she begins to unfold the nature and direction of this transformation by looking first at what needs to be *de*constructed:

> The first task, clearly, is to detach the sense of identity from the descriptions of yourself. This does not mean to find *another* description of you that would be the correct one. It means to realize that there is *no* description of *you*. That which is called by your name—your body, your history, your personality, your feelings—none of that is ultimately "you." Whatever is capable of being described and distinguished from other descriptions, all of that is to be stripped off so that the remaining selfhood may be called "naked," as it often is in the mystical traditions.[14]

One begins to leave the familiar psychological universe behind with the crucial discovery that the true self can never simply be a cleaned-up, high-functioning version of the "false self." It exists on a whole different level. Bruteau goes on to add, tellingly:

> Notice that this sense of identity is an internal sense of location or perspective, not a way of standing outside

of ourselves and looking back on ourselves. It is like knowing where you are by your sense of gravity or a sense of posture, or the point of view from which you see. *You are to coincide with the subjective act of being conscious, not to reflect on the fact of your being or of your being conscious.* [italics added][15]

In this one short sentence Bruteau offers the best description I have ever read of the classic domain of inner observation, distinguishing nicely between witnessing as "reflecting upon" and witnessing as "coinciding with." She then further clarifies that the chief operative in this distinction has something to do with *sensation:*

You learn it by a kind of practice, as you learn to balance yourself in walking or bicycle riding or swimming. You learn it as you learn to move one muscle without moving the one next to it, as in dancing or playing a musical instrument. You learn it as you learn, under biofeedback training, to produce alpha waves in your brain or to lower your blood pressure. It is a certain subtle sense of where you are or how you are, inside. You may "get the hang of it" suddenly or gradually.[16]

Thus, witnessing turns out not to be a mental operation at all. It is not about paying attention *to* anything, but rather about discovering an innate inner sense of gravity that offers itself as the seat of attention, the place one pays attention *from*. The access route is not through cognition, but through a much more somatic imprinting; Bruteau's analogies are all taken from the domain of physical training. Once one finds one's way to this inner center, it becomes the place to which one's deepest sense of selfhood automatically returns, like a pendulum coming to rest. From this place it is possible to "know" by coinciding with reality, not by thinking about it. Thus, the tedious self-consciousness and "double vision" of mentally centered witnessing drops out, to be replaced by a spontaneous inner freedom that can simultaneously rest in being while paying attention to the now. "Look, Ma, no hands!"—for the witnessing presence is held deeper, at the gravitational center of one's being, leaving the mind free to do what it does best: keep track of the temporal scene.

"Acquiring" Being

Though none of them say this directly, many teachers in the inner tradition hint broadly that the capacity to do this is not simply a technique to be learned. The capacity to "coincide with the subjective act of being conscious" (rather than merely falling into mental reflection) is itself a highly energized spiritual state and requires a significant degree of inner being (or "presence") in order to be sustained. This presence must be "accumulated," not merely mastered. Until a certain critical threshold is reached, one will inevitably slip back into mental operations because there is not yet enough inner force to stay present to being itself. In classic inner teaching, this capacity for sustained presence depends on the accumulation of what is known as "free attention"—that is, attention capable of reposing within that unified inner field I spoke of earlier ("quivering like a drop of mercury"), rather than being constantly drawn outward in identified reactions.

The great energy drain on our capacity for pure being is our well-engrained habit of, as Bruteau put it, "identifying with our descriptions"—that is, allowing our attention to flow automatically into the subject/object configuration rather than guarding it "within the heart," as Simeon the New Theologian admonishes. The problem is not simply that the descriptions are inadequate; the deeper problem is that this process itself is hugely entropic. The repetitive motion of finding oneself through identification (even with true and worthy descriptions) keeps the being energy just below the critical velocity needed to escape the gravitational field of narrative selfhood.

Thus, as Simeon the New Theologian observed (see page 75), the time-honored strategy for "finding one's way to the place where the heart is"—that is, the capacity to sustain witnessing presence from that inner center of gravity rather than from the mind—is simply *to let go of identifying*. Loose the bond and break the seals of the subject/object configuration of attention, and what emerges is a highly energized field of pure "free attention" that will eventually call to itself a new center of selfhood. Bruteau describes this relationship between withdrawing energy from the descriptors (or "predicates" as she calls them here) and reclaiming it as pure being in a passage of unparalleled beauty and clarity:

> When you are perfectly empty of all predicates—including the description of yourself as a "receiver"—then you are intensely full of pure "I am." And just as this point is reached, it explodes into the creative outpouring energy . . . I call this energy spondic because it pours out like a sacred libation, and this perfect liberty I call "creative freedom."[17]

Magnetic Center

Practitioners of Centering Prayer get an early jump on learning how to cut through this outflowing tendency of our attention. Since the prayer works entirely with "intention, not attention" (as Thomas Keating repeatedly emphasizes), there is no focal point for the attention, not even the breath or a mantra. Practitioners must learn early how to maintain their attention in (or more often, return it *to*) that inner, undifferentiated state.

Anything that serves as an object for the attention, no matter how pious or holy—a vision, intercessory prayer, an itch on your nose—is considered in this practice to be a "thought" and must be let go of. As practitioners gradually learn the art of withdrawing energy from all objects of attention, they are at the same time (and largely unbeknownst to themselves) developing an inner capacity to distinguish by feel the difference between attention *in* and attention *on*. Letting go is first and foremost a gesture—a subtle inner drop and release—and every opportunity to practice it strengthens the patterning.

I was several years into the practice of Centering Prayer before I came to appreciate the cumulative effect of this patterning. Like most beginners, I thought that the aim in Centering Prayer was to let go of my thoughts so that God could "fill" me with his presence. One day I suddenly realized that the God story was the sideshow and the letting go was the main event. That was when the practice flipped for me, as I recognized that thoughts were not the obstacle; they were the *raw material*, as every opportunity to practice releasing that focal point for attention deepened the reservoir of "free attention" within me and strengthened the signal of the homing beacon of my heart.

Sooner or later a tipping point is reached (often first experienced in the synergy of an intensive immersion retreat) when the strength of this signal becomes stronger than the attraction exerted by the thoughts. When a thought arises at the surface of the mind, a countering pull from the depths becomes so strong that letting go is effortless; in fact, it is impossible to do otherwise. At about this time, typically, one also begins to experience this "tug" outside of the prayer period itself, as events of daily life offer themselves as reminders of (rather than distractions from) the deeper yearning of the heart.

In *Centering Prayer and Inner Awakening*, I identified this "tug" as the activation in oneself of what I call "magnetic center." The term itself comes from the Gurdjieff Work, and what Gurdjieff meant by it is as follows: under the normal circumstances of "ordinary unconsciousness," every whim of life, every attraction and aversion, creates a new direction in our being as our attention swings around like a weathercock. But as magnetic center begins to develop, we acquire a root within us that can stay connected to our deepest spiritual aim and steer a true course increasingly independent of reactivity to external circumstances. A "something" begins to quicken in us. My discovery of the link between that "tug to center" of Centering Prayer and magnetic center as described by Gurdjieff was my own breakthrough moment in Centering Prayer and is confirmed by Simeon the New Theologian's teachings that letting go of all "passionate attachments" does in fact strengthen attention of the heart.[18] Contemporary neuroscience seems to be confirming this as well, as evidence continues to accumulate that the "letting go" motion (relaxing, unbracing, inner softening) does indeed seem to catalyze a mind/heart entrainment from which both personal well-being and an enhanced creativity emerge as the fruits.[19]

In the traditional sense of the term (implying an alert attention and conscious mental observer), Centering Prayer would not pass muster as a witnessing practice. But if what I am seeing here is correct, it does indeed have a key piece to contribute to our understanding of witnessing—in fact, it may well hold the missing piece of the puzzle. Its great strength as a practice is that it begins to build (or quicken) within a person a new center of gravity through which that traditional cul-de-sac of most witnessing practice—the mind spying on itself—can be surmounted by a new ability to remain rooted in being through sensation, not reflection. This is a huge milestone. It begins to approximate the capacity for that ancient desideratum of the Song of Songs: "I sleep, but my heart is awake." All that now remains is to transpose the usual seat of one's identity from the narrative self to this native ground of witnessing presence.

Welcoming

In this regard, I would like to offer a few comments about the Welcoming Practice—or Welcoming Prayer, as the Contemplative Outreach leadership now prefers to call it. At the request of this leadership, I did change the title of the chapter in *Centering Prayer and Inner Awakening* to reflect this new dispensation, but I now regret the decision. By anyone's definition, welcoming is indeed a practice—in fact, one of, if not *the* strongest and potentially life-changing in the repertory of Christian spiritual practices. By the same degree that it is seen as a prayer and not a practice, one loses sight of the radically transformative witnessing component at its core.

Mary Mrozowski knew what she was about when she put the practice together in the late 1980s through a skillful interweaving of three threads: the focusing work she was learning through biofeedback training, the attitude of deep inner surrender coming to her from Jean-Pierre de Caussade's seventeenth-century spiritual classic *Abandonment to Divine Providence,* and her own synthesis of Thomas Keating's teachings on the "false self system." Its three-step methodology is intended to take the "letting go" gesture imprinted during the time of Centering Prayer and carry it actively into daily life.

The first step, "focus (or sink in)," anchors you solidly in the realm of sensation. The instructions are very clear that, when knocked off course by an emotional or physical upset, you immediately become present to the upset *as physical sensation in your body*. There are no stories and commentaries and no instructions (at this point) to shift the physical energy, only to stay present to it. This all-important first step ensures that there will be no mental dissociation—one piece of the mind commenting on another, the usual bête noire of witnessing. The attention shifts lower in the body and is carried by sensation, the true seat of inner witnessing.

In the second step—welcoming—you unconditionally accept the reality of this sensation sharing the Now with you: be it physical pain, mental pain, emotional distress, or giddy self-satisfaction.[20] It is always the *sensation* you are accepting—the emotional signature of the fear, pain, joy, anger—and never the external situation itself. This is the reason I prefer for people to name the sensation lightly—"Welcome, fear," "Welcome, pain," and so forth—rather than merely saying "Welcome," which all too often leads to the impression that one is welcoming the outer circumstances rather than the inner ones.

In this alignment—grounded in sensation, unconditionally present to the energetic disturbance in your field of consciousness—you have "backed" into witnessing consciousness in a full and authentic way. "You" as pure consciousness have trumped "you" as the victim of any story or situation. And in this pure witnessing position, connected to sensation but separated from story, the inner shift can be extremely powerful. Sometimes you can literally feel the energy that was bound up in identification break free and reconfigure itself as pure spondic energy, exactly as described by Beatrice Bruteau a few pages ago. (One of my students likened it to opening the cap on a vacuum-sealed container.) In that moment an infusion of pure being energy floods your body, and your ability to "coincide with the subjective act of being conscious" is incrementally reinforced.

That is why the instruction now given as step two in the Contemplative Outreach revised guidelines strikes me as still way too vague. The guideline now reads: "Welcome the Divine

Indwelling in the feelings, emotions, thoughts, commentaries, or sensation in your body." To be sure, this is a great improvement over the earlier version—"Welcome the Holy Spirit present in this distressing emotion or situation." But depending on whether you interpret "The Divine Indwelling" as simply a synonym for the Holy Spirit (rather than as an innate attribute of embodied consciousness), you are still merely replacing one story with another ("This situation stinks, but I know the Holy Spirit is in here somewhere"), and this misunderstanding can all too easily lead right back into those traditional inner stances of quietism and passive victimhood in which acquiescence is mistaken for true spiritual surrender.

Rather, it is better formulated as "By the power of the Divine Indwelling active within me, I unconditionally embrace this moment, no matter its physical or psychological content." And by this same indwelling strength, once inner wholeness is restored, I then choose how to deal with the outer situation, be it by acceptance or by spirited resistance. If the latter course is chosen, the actions taken—reflecting that higher coherence of witnessing presence—will have a greater effectiveness, bearing the right force and appropriate timing that Buddhist teaching classically designates as "skillful means."

Unconditional Presence

"As your being increases, your receptivity to higher meaning increases. As your being decreases, the old meanings return."[21] This comment by the British esotericist Maurice Nicoll concisely summarizes much of what has been under discussion in this chapter. Since this material is still largely unfamiliar territory to many Christian contemplatives, perhaps it would be helpful to conclude this section with a brief recap of the major points I have been trying to make.

Witnessing, or inner observation, is an activity that requires as its precondition the attainment of a certain critical threshold of "being." Otherwise it will inevitably slip into the mental mode: reflecting *on,* rather than coinciding *with.* This being (or presence) is "accumulated"—or activated, if you prefer—within a person basically by breaking the bonds that cause it to become instantly bound up in identification. And identification, you remember, is not simply an attachment, or a "bad" spiritual habit: it reflects an underlying arrangement of attention in a subject/object configuration, whereby attention is drawn outward and seeks identity in the objects—or "predicates," as Bruteau calls them. When this unconscious outward movement is reversed, a flood of energy is released within that allows "coinciding with the subjective act of being conscious" to become a lived reality within oneself—a vibratory field of knowingness. This is the real meaning of the term "attention of the heart."

In its teaching and methodology, Centering Prayer contributes two of the foundational skills required to sustain this more somatic form of witnessing. While not commonly thought of as a witnessing practice, it does incrementally develop an ability to hold attention as a unified field rather than a subject/object polarity. And it imprints the basic gesture through which this "attention of the heart" most naturally arises: through a letting go of "thoughts"—that is, packets of consciousness formatted in that polarized subject/object way (right up to and including the "thought" of self). As such, it lays down a strong practical foundation for making the transition from a narrative sense of selfhood into the "creative freedom" of the unitive self. The tools are all there in the Centering Prayer teaching. The challenge for an upcoming generation of practitioners is to more fully utilize them.

CHAPTER 5

Further to Simeon the New Theologian

I realize that at this point we have several threads running in this discussion: nonduality, attention of the heart, witnessing presence, Centering Prayer. In this chapter I will attempt to pull some of these threads together by making one more pass through Simeon the New Theologian's "Three Methods of Attention and Prayer," this time from the perspective of what it may reveal about Simeon's grasp of nondual consciousness.

As you may have gathered, Simeon's essay has been on my radar screen for a long time now. I first met up with it back in the early 1980s through Jacob Needleman's iconic book *Lost Christianity*.[1] Simeon evidently made a powerful impression on Needleman, and through Needleman he made a powerful impression on me. I quickly located the essay and worked my way carefully through it, immediately recognizing its powerful implications for my own developing practice of Centering Prayer. It has been a mainstay of my teaching ever since.

As a longtime student of the Gurdjieff Work, Needleman was naturally drawn to Simeon's meticulous understanding of attention, a subject that is front and center in the Work but rarely discussed (at least directly) elsewhere in the spiritual literature of the West. Needleman was the first to alert me to this piece as a groundbreaking study in the phenomenology of attention, and to the centrality of the heart in the emergence of this other kind of attention, attention of a whole different order of magnitude that makes possible an entirely different kind of perceptivity.

As I have stated before, I believe that the West's key contribution to the understanding of nondual perception is that this highest-order ("third tier") level of consciousness is not a mere extension of the cognitive line—that is, the mind. It implies and requires the shift to an entirely different operating system, which is *anatomically* located in the heart—or better yet, in the mind in entrainment with the heart. Apart from this shift in the hardwiring of perception, nonduality is not attainable, let alone sustainable. So let's revisit the essay with this proposition in mind.

If we can depart from a strictly chronological progression through the text in favor of an overview of its major insights vis-à-vis what we would now call "nondual awakening," here are my three top takeaways:

First, Simeon implicitly recognizes that the teaching of Jesus emerges from a higher level of consciousness that is inaccessible to human beings in their ordinary state of mind. This revelation emerges as the surprising conclusion to what at first appears to be a lengthy digression on the spiritual virtues of conscience, sobriety, and obedience before he finally unveils his third method of attention and prayer. But digression it definitely is not, for these are the fundamental outer prerequisites for establishing a stable inner attention, and without this inner attention, any attempt to put on the mind of Christ will be futile:

> In a word, he who does not have attention in himself and does not guard his mind, cannot become pure in heart and cannot see God. He who does not have attention

in himself cannot be poor in spirit, cannot weep and be contrite, nor be gentle and meek, nor hunger and thirst after righteousness, nor be merciful, nor suffer persecution for righteousness sake. Speaking generally, it is impossible to gain virtue in any other way except through this kind of attention.[2]

If one aspires to live the Beatitudes or any of the other sublime Gospel teachings, it is first necessary to establish a direct inner resonance with the level of consciousness from which they emerge. Simeon does not say this explicitly, but the implication is hard to miss. And guarding attention within the heart, as he sees it, is the linchpin to the entire operation.

Second, he recognizes very keenly that this "higher order consciousness" (if it's permissible to reframe it in these terms) is not awakened by traditional cataphatic methods of prayer and self-examination. It is accessed neither through concentration of affectivity (the first method of attention and prayer) or through mentally based mindfulness (the second method). In Gurdjieffian language, it cannot be had by either the emotional center or the intellectual center working in isolation. Rather, it is a whole different mode of perception activated by a radically different configuration and deployment of attention. The essence of this reconfiguration lies in the shift from "attention on" to "attention *in*." Only the heart is capable of holding this other attentional field.

In Simeon's second method of attention and prayer, we are in the classic domain of self-reflexive consciousness, the default operating system of the mind. It is the system that basically runs the show throughout the entire gamut of first- and second-tier levels of consciousness, plying its faithful but pedantic "perception through differentiation" program in order to measure, evaluate, and manipulate the outer world from its hermetically sealed inner command post. We noted in the last chapter how Simeon quickly nails this system on its two major liabilities: its shadow side in vainglory (in other words, the ego's illusion that it is making spiritual progress) and its vulnerability to blindsiding by forces emerging from the unconscious. While I suggested the term "dissociation" as a modern equivalent for Simeon's somewhat startling observation that this blindsiding happens "because [a man] remains in his head, whereas evil thoughts are generated in the heart," there is another possibility as well, even more broadly suggested in Simeon's commentary: the person is physically off-balance inside, holding his or her center of gravity too high, well above where the action is actually taking place. "Such a man is like one fighting his enemies at night, in the dark," Simeon observes: "He hears their voices and suffers their blows, but cannot see who they are."[3] Again, there is an implicit awareness that one must *descend,* concentrate the attention at a point closer to the physical center of one's being, in order to escape the incessantly circular and vicarious machinations of the mind.

Third, the distinguishing features of this third method of attention, as enumerated by Simeon, have striking overlaps with what we would nowadays call the readily identifiable features of nondual consciousness. Simeon names three of these, you recall.

> You should observe freedom from all cares, not only cares about bad and vain but even about good things.

Simeon is clearly indicating here a state of consciousness that lives beyond "good and bad," beyond judgment. It has ceased trying to replace negativity with positivity (the classic hallmark of an immature spiritual practice still firmly grounded in binary thinking)[4] and has learned to live equidistant from both, in that liminal space "where all your deeds and words, each truth, each lie, die in unjudging love" (in the beautiful words of poet Dylan Thomas).[5] Nonjudging mind is a classic attribute of nondual perception.

> Your conscience should be clear in all things, so that it denounces you in nothing.

Conscience is the mirror in which the divine light is reflected. When it becomes clouded or co-opted, attention of the heart can no longer be maintained.

It's one of the most universal and painful of human experiences to get crosswise with your conscience, and with even rudimentary witnessing skills, what almost immediately comes to the forefront is that bedeviling sense of twoness. At one level, that smaller self caught up in the desire at hand is emphatically justifying, defending, yearning, and posturing. And all the while the other voice merely looks on, gently whispering, "You think so, eh?" It can be drowned, overridden, or rejected, but the twoness remains—and will remain, until the broken field is restored in the only way it possibly can be, in favor of conscience. All the while, the heart's function as an organ of spiritual perception is effectively disabled by the struggle. That is why the spiritual traditions of both the East and the West have placed such emphasis on total transparency with one's abba, guru, or spiritual guide, for a house divided against itself will fall back into the gravitational field of duality.

> And you should have a complete absence of passionate attachment, so that your thought inclines to nothing worldly.

As we have discovered already, the phrase "passionate attachment" is actually a redundancy. All passion is by definition *already* attachment—or more specifically, the psychic energy uselessly bound up and squandered in attachment. Simeon is advising us here to plug the energy leaks.

If you can pass beyond your immediate, conditioned reaction to the phrase "so that your mind inclines to nothing worldly" (i.e., don't think about bad, sinful, sensual things), you'll see that what Simeon is really describing here is a configuration of attention that does not "incline"—that is, allow itself to run out to any objects whatsoever. This kind of attention has learned how to remain collected within itself, not being drawn back into that subject/object polarity that is the drive shaft of binary perception. In this sense "worldly" describes *any* thought that furnishes a focal point for the attention, not merely "bad" or "sinful" thoughts. (That contingency has already been dealt with in Simeon's first instruction.) In addition to comprising a defining feature of Simeon's attention of the heart, it is also a good working definition of *objectless awareness,* that radically different way of organizing the perceptual field that furnishes the neurological gateway to nondual perception.

Nonjudgment, an undivided viewing screen, and *objectless awareness*—these are the three hallmarks of this other mode of awareness, which Simeon calls "attention of the heart." They are simultaneously the fruits of this attainment and the pathway to attaining it. And it's hard to deny that they are pretty close ringers for what we would nowadays call nondual attainment.

A Final Caveat, However . . .

In both of my earlier passes through Simeon, I have commented on how closely the method of Centering Prayer parallels Simeon's third method of attention and prayer. In practicing Centering Prayer, one will be working repeatedly with nonjudgment, nonattachment, and restoring the field of open awareness after it has been co-opted by "passionate attachment" to an object of attention (known in Centering Prayer teaching as a "thought"). In this way, Centering Prayer definitely resonates with the overall spirit of Simeon's instructions and offers an immediate meditational access route for putting theses precepts into practice.

But this is as far as I would want to push it. Beyond here, any comparisons between Centering Prayer and the great Orthodox tradition of Prayer of the Heart quickly become simplistic, perhaps dangerously so. It is true that Centering Prayer closely replicates the underlying kenotic thread of the Orthodox tradition. But it leaves untouched that entire other dimension of the practice: the direct work with sensation as an access point to heart consciousness. For clearly, the repeated reminder to "put the mind in the heart" is not *simply* about releasing attachment; it is also about concentrating attention at a single point so that it becomes strong enough to enter the heart through direct sensation rather than mental or emotional operations. This is essentially the practice Robert Sardello was describing in his chapter "The Silence of the Heart" (in his book *Silence,* mentioned earlier, where he draws on the power of a developed, sensation-based attention to enter the vibrational field of the heart and discover there those currents of "pure intimacy"). In this way, and only in this way, the distinction between being conscious *of* the heart and being conscious *in* the heart begins to become clear. It is clear that for these Orthodox spiritual masters "concentrating the attention in the heart" is a *strong, sensation-based physical practice,* not just a spiritual attitude. If we miss this crucial distinction and think that Centering Prayer is "the same as" the ancient Hesychastic tradition of Prayer of the Heart, we have made a serious miscalculation.[6]

I raise this point partly in the interest of full disclosure, lest in the excitement of noting these parallels between Centering Prayer and the great Orthodox tradition of Prayer of the Heart, we also sail right through some telling differences. But I raise it as well because, since Centering Prayer is so clearly in so many ways the most recent flowering of an ancient Christian kenotic lineage, it is important to be aware of the original, more comprehensive understanding of kenotic practice as grounded in sensation, not simply in a theological attitude. Whether this wider acknowledgment is possible within the strict givens of the method, I do not know. But it is certainly a growing edge for Centering Prayer, which I will be circling back to several times in the course of this book.

CHAPTER 6

Centering Prayer: Perspectives from the Neurosciences

In the past decade there has been a veritable explosion of information in the emerging field of neuroscience. With the aid of technologies, such as EEG (electroencephalography) and fMRI (functional magnetic resonance imaging), scientists are able to map with ever-increasing accuracy the picture of "your brain in meditation," providing a powerful second line of bearing on the claims long advanced by the sacred traditions that a regular practice of meditation changes the brain in positive and significant ways.

The HeartMath Institute got an early jump on the fMRI research and has continued to dominate the popular end of the field in exactly the area where our own concerns in this book will ultimately lie: the question of brain/heart connectivity. But within the greater neuroscience community the institute remains something of a maverick, and its boldly presented research has yet to cross-pollinate with the data being generated according to the more rigorous standards of traditional academic research. Here the research continues to focus on the brain alone (not yet brain/heart connectivity), with the proximate goal of developing increasingly more sophisticated ways of identifying the specific regions involved in brain-wave generation and their patterns of connectivity.

For reasons that will become apparent shortly, it's worth mentioning that this more academic end of the spectrum also tends to be heavily Buddhist-influenced—in no small part because the cultivation of this research reflects a long-standing personal priority of the Dalai Lama himself. Through an on-going series of high-level conferences and academic collaborations stretching back now for almost thirty years,[1] he has deliberately nurtured a rich partnership between the best of academic neuroscience and the best of traditional Tibetan Buddhist wisdom on the phenomenology of consciousness. The hugely popular spin-off of all this, of course, is our current cultural fascination with mindfulness and a spate of best sellers detailing how to "train your mind, change your brain."[2] Not surprisingly, given the initial impetus behind the movement, many of the top players in the neuroscience field (certainly, to date, the most high-profile ones) reflect a strongly Buddhist perspective, including Jon Kabat-Zinn, Richard Davidson, Daniel Brown, Sharon Begley, Matthieu Ricard, Antoine Lutz, and Evan Thompson.

The implications of these developments for a better understanding of Christianity's own contemplative heritage are huge. With steadily growing leaps in the technology, we can expect within the foreseeable future to have a much better picture of what Centering Prayer looks like from perspectives within neuroscience. This picture should help us to situate it better within the overall taxonomy of meditation practices and to validate (or as the case may be, *invalidate*) some of the claims that have been made on its behalf. More broadly, it opens the gateway to a far more comprehensive understanding of the Christian "way of the heart" as an embodied reality.

But while these breakthroughs may be just around the

corner, there are still significant hurdles to be navigated before Centering Prayer really shows up on the neuroscience radar screen. The first of these, which I raised already in my introduction, has been a general underappreciation within the wider neuromeditation community of the distinctive features of Centering Prayer and the spiritual principles on which it rests. This is perhaps not surprising in a field where the conversation to date has been so heavily dominated by Buddhist models. If the awareness even dawns that Christianity has its own meditation tradition, the tendency is to assume that it conforms to a standard mindfulness model: that there is a "generic" entry-level meditation, and Centering Prayer is simply the Christian name for it.

A flagrant example of this kind of hybridizing confusion is seen in Andrew Newberg's recent best seller, *How God Changes Your Brain*. Newberg is a respected neuroscientist and his intention in this book is certainly laudable: to cast as wide a net as possible of simple, useful practices that will allow immediate access to the neurological benefits set in motion by a regular practice of meditation. But his "slightly modified" version of "the Centering Prayer"[3] leaves the practice bearing very little resemblance to its ostensible namesake. Stepping off from the initial misassumption that Centering Prayer is "like other forms of mindfulness meditation"[4] and that therefore the goal is to "allow your mind to reflect on all the qualities associated with a particular idea," he proposes the following expanded guidelines:

1. First, identify what your objective is (finding inner peace, experiencing compassion for others, receiving God's presence, etc.). Or if you prefer, pick a particularly meaningful quote, poem, or passage from a book.

2. When you have found a concept or passage you wish to explore on a deeper, intuitive level, sit down in a comfortable chair. Close your eyes, breathe slowly and deeply, and make sure all of your tensions are gone.

3. Now focus your awareness on the selected object of contemplation. Do not repeat any words or expressions to yourself. Just be aware of all the thoughts, perceptions, feelings, images, and memories that your contemplation evokes.

4. Notice how you are feeling. Are you happy? Joyful? Sad? Now bring your attention back to your goal, and again watch what feelings and thoughts begin to emerge.

5. If your mind wanders too far away, gently return your awareness by taking several deep breaths, bringing your focus back to your goal, phrase, or prayer. Again, let your thoughts wander wherever they want to go.

6. If the object of your contemplation becomes vague or disappears, simply watch what happens next. Don't "do" anything or "make" anything happen—just let the experience naturally unfold. After several minutes return again to the object of your contemplation.

7. Continue this process for a minimum of twenty minutes. Then slowly open your eyes. Remain silent for two more minutes while you take slow, deep breaths and yawns.[5]

By my count, this "slightly modified" version of Centering Prayer contains at least ten major violations of the method of Centering Prayer. The combined effect is to transform it back into a generic mindfulness practice fluctuating between con-centrative meditation (focus on an object) and "awareness" meditation. Gone is every trace of the kenotic epicenter with its signature gesture of release. Gone as well is any awareness that the practice is not goal-oriented and that the attention is not object-oriented. If researchers work with *this* version of the practice, they will certainly identify a characteristic (and no doubt familiar) brain-wave signature. But they will not be measuring Centering Prayer. Until the method can be named and recognized for what it actually is, it will be impossible to acquire accurate neurological data.

A second reason why the data is challenging to retrieve, is, frankly, that not all who claim to be practicing Centering Prayer are actually doing so—or at any rate, doing so with full understanding of the prayer's kenotic character. Until the gesture of release is well understood and firmly imprinted, the tendency of a practitioner will be to fixate on the sacred word, using it either as a stimulus for reflection, a mantra, or a mine-sweeper to drive away other thoughts. This obviously shifts the format of the prayer back to a concentrative practice, and if the practitioner happens at that time to be wired up to an EEG, the brain signature will not be noticeably different from that generated by any other form of concentrative practice.

The combination of these first two factors—the Buddhist skew of the models and the uneven understanding of the method even among Centering Prayer practitioners themselves—leads to the third limiting factor in any attempt to develop an accurate neurological picture of Centering Prayer: namely, that the data is still very limited. To date, the research pool has essentially been too poorly delimited and the measuring criteria too vague to yield statistically significant results.[6]

A New Viewing Platform

The picture may soon be shifting, however, with the release of research long in preparation by California neuroscientist

Michael Spezio and his Princeton-based colleague Brent Field, together with interspiritual consultant Andrew Dreitcer. Spezio is a professor of psychology at Scripps College and a longtime student of Thomas Keating. He has been following Centering Prayer for more than a decade now, both as a practitioner and as a research scientist, and his accumulated data on Centering Prayer practitioners is probably the largest and most carefully vetted body of information to date available. Working with state-of-the-art technologies unavailable even two years ago, he has been able to dissect the individual components of a given brain wave, editing out extraneous muscle movement and focusing in on patterns of *connectivity* (the sequence and ordering of brain regions involved in generating a specific brain-wave pattern). His colleague Field has meanwhile been conducting parallel research on a comparable group of Tibetan Buddhist practitioners ranging from those working basically with concentrative practices (*shamatha* and *vipassana*) to fifteen highly advanced practitioners whose principal practice tended toward *dzogchen* ("objectless awareness") The third member of their research team, Dreitcer, is an associate professor of theology at the Claremont School of Theology and a longtime participant in the Dalai Lama's Mind and Life Institute. The study is the first of its kind to directly pair a statistically significant body of Centering Prayer practitioners with a comparable body of Buddhist practitioners within an intentionally interdisciplinary and interspiritual framework.

Because the scheduled release date for this study is essentially concurrent with the publication of my own book, I was unable to work with an advanced copy of the report. This nonspecialist "trailer" is based on individual phone interviews plus an on-site tour of the research laboratory at Scripps College. While the picture here is thus admittedly incomplete, it seemed important to include at least a mention of it here, as it will almost certainly have a significant impact on how Centering Prayer is understood within the wider meditation community.

One of the most significant features of this new study is that it creates a much more comprehensive template on which to correlate the data. Rather than simply categorizing practices by name or by the spiritual tradition they belong to, it instead identifies four generic *types* of meditation practice to be tested in *both* research populations across a spectrum of proficiencies:

- concentrative practice
- receptive practice
- discursive meditation
- simple "at rest" state, eyes open and eyes closed

Readers will immediately note how this expanded model is already more amenable to Christian reference points, the first two categories figuring prominently in Thomas Keating's own conceptual road map and the third a staple of traditional monastic formation. For the purposes of this study, *concentrative practice* entails focused attention; *receptive practice* features the release of that object-oriented focus (informally described to me by both Spezio and Field as a "drop" into a different inner state). *Discursive meditation* entails language, visualization, and vocalization. (Centering Prayer participants were asked to recite the Lord's Prayer.) The fourth category is intended to test whether contemplative practitioners are at all different in their resting brain states compared to others.

In addition, the study tested for a fifth condition, "active listening with eyes closed," which served as an active control for the function of focused attention when contrasting attentive listening to Centering Prayer. This control condition, a standard procedure in any sound scientific research, is especially important in this particular study because of the wide-spread concentrative bias that interprets Centering Prayer as simply another form of attentional practice, similar to shamatha, for example.

"Deep Memory . . . Memory of Unity"

In large part, the initial impressions emerging from a very preliminary summary of the data are consistent with earlier research, their major contribution being to bring a new level of precision to the analysis. Concentrative practice, already extensively described in both the scientific and popular litera-ture, tends to stimulate the visual cortex and the parietal lobes, brain regions involved with focus, attention, and visualization. Not surprisingly, since Centering Prayer is an "eyes closed" meditation, practitioners (even immature ones, tending toward a more concentrative rendition of the practice) registered less activity in the visual cortex, and a somewhat higher level of alpha brain-wave activity than in a standard "mindfulness" model. With discursive meditation those areas of the brain controlling language (the frontal lobes) are engaged, and there is often an increase in external body movement, ranging from eye motion to actual gesticulation.

The real surprises came when the advanced practition-ers in both data pools were invited into receptive medita-tion. The movement into this mode came effortlessly, virtually instantaneously—clearly the fruit of long years of committed practice.[7] At this mature level, the meditation practices themselves bear some definite resonances across traditions. "I have seen moments where Centering Prayer looks like *dzogchen*," Field observes, "but it's hard to say whether this is superficial or part of the practice." This "drop" (explicitly characterized as such) from concentrative into receptive practice has been reported anecdotally by many mature Buddhist practitioners, perhaps most prominently by Sharon Salzberg in her personal account recorded in *Gethsemani Encounter*.[8] But it had not heretofore been observed within a specifically Christian meditational format.

Another surprising commonality when these highly advanced practitioners dropped into receptive meditation was at least a preliminary indication of hippocampus involvement, that very interior region of the brain controlling memory. But what kind of memory might this be since the more cognitive/ narrative memory driving one's usual sense of selfhood has been suspended in the meditation? Spezio is examining the data more closely to see whether memory structures, including the hippocampus, may indeed be being recruited by Centering Prayer and characterizes this possibility as perhaps a recovery of "deep memory . . . memory of unity."[9] This speculation takes on additional shades of meaning when you recall that one of the traditional definitions of mindfulness, curiously neglected in modern secular versions, is *remembrance*—something much more akin to traditional Christian notions of "recollection" than current secular definitions would indicate.[10]

And indeed, if the expectations of the studies prove to bear fruit, so it may appear neurologically. Whether or not these adepts are remembering unity, they are clearly remembering *something*—or perhaps simply resting in a state of profound remembrance. One way or another, some aspect of deep memory is being neurologically engaged.

Overall, what seemed to be the hallmark of the mature practitioners (in both camps) was that stabilized state of recollection or "living remembrance." At this level of mastery, meditation is no longer even really a *practice,* but simply a natural outflow of a heart attunement already fully stabilized. As Field observed eloquently of one mature research participant: "He is someone who has cultivated in himself the complete orientation to the divine. Meditation is simply the celebration of this." In this light, the initial similarity between Buddhist and Centering Prayer adepts may have less to do with the specific methods of meditation used and more to do with where those years of faithful practice have ultimately brought them: to transcendence of ego-self and awakening of the heart. In fact, states Spezio, "these studies of practice, absent clear evidence of an integrated life for others, are completely meaningless. The practices in contemplation must extend to lived experience, to actions for and with others, or they are not practices that we are all interested in."[11]

But of course, isn't this what Thomas Keating has been saying all along? "The fruits of Centering Prayer are found in daily life." Neuroscience can measure a slice of this deep interior unity as it transpires on the meditation cushion, certainly enough to corroborate that there is indeed water in the well. But the proof of the pudding lies in the integrated personhood.

Unity Attained

In a way, the most significant question raised by the study is the one that it does *not* raise—not directly, anyway. If such states of profound spiritual unity do in fact exist and can be measured by EEG, is such spiritual attainment a function of the meditation practices alone, or does it require the supportive participation of the entire ethical and devotional matrix in which these practices are embedded? Given the contemporary trend toward the secular repackaging of spiritual practice, it is a timely concern.

While that question is beyond the scope of a strictly scientific study, it is very much on the minds of Michael Spezio, Brent Field, and Andrew Dreitcer. In a substantial scholarly monograph, essentially a companion piece to their research paper, they once again team up to articulate some of those ethical and spiritual dimensions to which the neuroscience data implicitly speaks.[12]

What tends to go missing when spiritual practice is secularized, the authors argue, is precisely that rich and multidimensional context in which mindfulness as "present moment awareness" flows seamlessly into mindfulness as authentic spiritual remembrance. In a secular container, mindfulness tends to become privatized, appearing as a set of personal coping skills or personal wellness benefits. But in its original spiritual setting mindfulness is irreducibly relational and ethical. Its fruits are not wellness, personal longevity, or neuroplasticity. They are compassion, equanimity, and love. In contrast to the various secular and scientific models (extensively documented in this article), the spiritual model gives central place to mindfulness as "the awareness of and familiarity with an ethically oriented ultimate reality that makes human wholeness possible."[13] It is only against this backdrop that notions such as "remembrance" and "unity" make any sense whatsoever.

As an important first step toward reclaiming this wider understanding of mindfulness as remembrance, the authors explore the crucial importance of *imitatio* ("imitation," as in *imitatio Christi,* "the imitation of Christ"), a foundational spiritual practice in both Eastern and Western traditions and a generally unappreciated commonality between them. Beginning with the grateful "calling to mind" of one's teacher, *imitatio* progresses toward an ever-deepening assimilation of that teacher and teaching into the student's being until at last the two lives become fused in a single stream of living presence.[14] Mindfulness as attention is gradually transformed into mindfulness as participation in a living relational field, simultaneously intimate and cosmic.

Thomas Keating has himself suggested the term "heartfulness" as a complement to the more secularized "mindfulness," encompassing those fuller dimensions of compassion, remembrance, and relationality. His suggestion has found strong support among the interspiritual participants in his on-going Snowmass dialogues[15] and is already well established within the Centering Prayer network. In addition to highlighting the empathetic and relational dimensions of this mode of presence, it also creates a strong bridge to the rich Christian lineage of prayer of the heart we have been exploring in this section of the book.

While reestablishing this wider spiritual context is certainly helpful to a fuller understanding of mindfulness practice, with Centering Prayer I believe it is essential, for apart from its kenotic grounding, the practice remains basically unintelligible. In secular mindfulness there is at least a motivational initial entry gate through which some benefit is to be accrued thereby, be it stress reduction, better attentional skills, or lower blood pressure. But kenosis and self-surrender really have no cultural starting points; apart from a direct apprehension of the great mystical traditions of *imitatio* and remembrance in which the practice is embedded, Centering Prayer remains stubbornly counterintuitive.

Is it possible that neuroscience might someday join in this fuller exploration of what it looks like empirically to "put the mind in the heart"? In one sense, that seems like an odd question to be raising here, for that research has already been well begun with the HeartMath Institute and its extensive fMRI documentation of brain/heart entrainment. But as I mentioned at the beginning of the chapter, the problem from an academic perspective is that the two research communities are not working on the same levels, so comparing the data is bit like comparing apples and oranges. From the start the HeartMath Institute has chosen to operate outside the academic box, gearing its research toward a wider audience and more immediately practical objectives.[16] This means that its research is not bound to the same verification protocols as are standard operating procedure in academic circles—and hence, for better or worse, it has no official standing in the official academic dialogue. This is clearly a loss from my point of view, since in principle the HeartMath Institute has a far better intuitive grasp of the terrain delineated by prayer of the heart and the Christian kenotic approach to nonduality than does the still Buddhist-dominated field of academic neuroscience. For HeartMath's initial groundbreaking discoveries to gain widespread scientific credibility, the research would most likely need to be independently replicated within established academic research laboratories following standard research protocols.

At present, according to Michael Spezio, there are only a few laboratories possessing the capacity to fully conduct such research, which requires simultaneously synchronized, high-resolution fMRI of both the heart and the brain together. But there *are* a few (three by Spezio's present count), and more will follow. And as a growing appreciation of heartfulness within the neuromeditation community encourages a shift in the focus of the research from brain alone to brain/heart connectivity, the data will begin to fall into place to evaluate Christianity's stubborn mystical intuition that nondual attainment (as we would language it nowadays) is not merely a new level of consciousness but a new *seat* of consciousness.

PART THREE

The *Cloud* of *Unknowing* Revisited

Centering into The Cloud

It's been more than forty years now since Thomas Keating, at the time abbot of Saint Joseph's Abbey in Spencer, Massachusetts, first set the Centering Prayer ball in motion with his famous challenge during a monastic chapter meeting: "Is it not possible to put the essence of the Christian contemplative path into a meditation method accessible to modern people living in the world?" Dismayed by what he saw as the growing defection of young Christian seekers to Eastern meditation paths, Dom Thomas invited the assistance of his monastic brethren in unearthing the treasure buried in their own Christian backyard.

One of the monks, Father William Meninger, took him up on the challenge. Returning to his well-thumbed copy of that fourteenth-century spiritual classic *The Cloud of Unknowing*, he opened to chapter 7, where he immediately located the paragraph that in short order would become the cornerstone of the method of Centering Prayer. In the midst of a discussion as to why many words are not necessary in prayer, but only a "naked intent direct to God," this anonymous English contemplative advises:

And if you desire to have this aim concentrated and expressed in a single word so that you are better able to
grasp it, take but one short word of a single syllable. This
is better than two, for it better accords with the work
of the spirit. Such a word is the word GOD or the word
LOVE. Choose whichever one you prefer, or if you like,
choose another that suits your taste, provided that it is
one syllable. And clasp this word tightly to your heart
so that it never leaves it no matter what might happen.[1]

And that, essentially, is what Centering Prayer practitioners
have been doing ever since.

Initially called "The Prayer of the Cloud," this no-frills
method of Christian meditation began to be offered to
retreatants at Saint Joseph's Abbey during the early 1970s—
at first only to clergy, but soon afterward to laypeople also.
In very short order it jumped the walls of the monastery, and
rebaptized as Centering Prayer, it went on to establish itself as
a powerful lay grassroots initiative. By the early 1980s the need
for some institutional infrastructure to manage growth and
maintain teaching standards within this burgeoning network
became clear, and Contemplative Outreach was formally established in 1983. Over these past thirty years it has grown
steadily into an international membership organization, now
several hundred thousand strong.

Now all of this is familiar history to longtime practitioners
of Centering Prayer, and as I write these words in the midst
of Contemplative Outreach's thirtieth anniversary commem-
orations, these commendable achievements are being duly
celebrated. But what really interests me in all this is its less
obvious corollary: that we now have a forty-year track record
of people in substantial number who have taken to heart *The
Cloud*'s core instructions and wrestled with them twice daily

on their meditation mats. If nothing else, that is quite a data bank! And it opens up a whole new avenue of inquiry into *The Cloud,* heretofore simply unavailable.

I say this because *The Cloud* is a mystical text, and like most mystical texts it can only ultimately be accessed at the level of consciousness from which it was written. "Like attracts like," as the old hermetic saying goes; the best way to engage a text written from a state of deep contemplative stillness is to match that state as closely as you can in yourself by meditating your way into the text rather than immediately having at it with your analytical mind. And there are things about *The Cloud* which, frankly, have stumped scholars for years, because these things only become apparent when the real meaning emerges out of the practice itself.

For example, *The Cloud* is usually regarded by scholars as a classic example of Christian affective mysticism, located squarely within the lineage flowing out of Pseudo Dionysius and down through the great river of monastic love mysticism, reaching its full flowering in the works of those great twelfth-century Cistercian masters, Bernard of Clairvaux and Richard of Saint Victor. The program here is basically "spiritual union through the transformation of eros." The heart's smoldering fires of erotic desire are fanned into full flame while at the same time being redirected away from earthly objects and toward heavenly ones—till at last, affectivity implodes into mystical marriage. It is a bold and effusive pathway, and at first *The Cloud* does indeed seem to fit right in. A statement like the celebrated "God may be reached and held close by means of love, but by means of thought never" (6-3)[2] would seem to clinch the case that this author is advocating a departure from the cerebral into the affective realms. And certainly his oft-repeated instruction to "lift up your heart with a meek stirring of love" and his specific counsel that "you are to strike that

thick cloud of unknowing with a sharp dart of longing love"
(6-4) would seem to be completely self-explanatory. How
could this be anything other than affectivity?

But then what do you do with *Cloud* 3-5 when the author
emphatically affirms "No matter what you do, this darkness
and this cloud is between you and your God and because of it
you can neither see Him clearly with your reason in the light
of understanding, *nor can you feel Him with your affection in
the sweetness of God*"? (Emphasis added.) Or in chapter 16,
describing Mary Magdalene as a model of the contemplative
transformation he has in mind: "Instead, she hung up her love
and her longing desire in this cloud of unknowing and learned
to love a thing she might never see clearly in this life, either by
the light of understanding of her *reason nor by a true feeling of
sweet love in her affection*" (16-5, emphasis added). Clearly,
the kind of love this author has in mind is of a fundamentally
different quality from what we usually mean by affectivity.
And rather than concentrating it on a holy object, we will see
shortly how he proposes to *dispense with objects altogether*!
If this is monastic love mysticism, it is certainly an unusual
version of it.

Out of my own three decades of experience in Centering Prayer, what I will shortly be proposing as the essence of
my argument here is that "love" indeed has nothing to do
with affectivity in the usual sense of the word. It is rather the
author's nearest equivalent term to describe what we would
nowadays call *nondual perception anchored in the heart*. And
he is indeed correct in calling it "love" because the energetic
bandwidth in which the heart works is *intimacy*, the capacity
to perceive things from the inside by coming into sympathetic
resonance with them. In contrast to the mind, which perceives
through discrimination and delineation, the heart takes its
bearings directly from the whole, through a process that scientists nowadays describe as "holographic resonance." Imag-

ine trying to describe that in the fourteenth century! The author here is not talking about affection; centuries ahead of his times, he is groping for metaphors to describe an entirely different mode of perceptivity.

Now, I know that what I just said there is a huge leap. Don't worry; I will be unpacking it in painstaking detail over the next few chapters. For now, the point I want to make is merely that I didn't come to this insight by scholarly analysis and deduction, but through thirty years of sitting on my meditation cushion. Like other seasoned practitioners of Centering Prayer, I have often experienced that mysterious golden tenderness that seems to be the signature energy field of Centering Prayer—pure intimacy, without any cause or object. I know exactly why the author characterizes it as "love," and why it is indeed a love that has nothing to do with emotion or affectivity in the usual sense of those words. I know also why he calls this meeting ground between the realms a "cloud"— and why this term is not simply a metaphor for the classic *via negativa*, or way of unknowing, but a very precise analogy for a kind of diffuse awareness in which attention no longer flows mechanically from subject to object and perception happens in a whole different way. I have experienced this myself, many times, during Centering Prayer—but only when I actually *do* the practice and let those alluring magnets for my attention float on by. And I am absolutely certain that I would have no idea apart from having done this practice what the author of *The Cloud* was talking about.

What I am proposing here, then, is to establish an intentional feedback loop between *The Cloud* and this interpretive data bank generated by forty years of committed Centering Prayer practitioners. If, as I suspect, Centering Prayer has indeed been laying the neurological groundwork for the transition into this other, nondual mode of perception—a core thesis of this book—then it stands to reason that insights harvested from the meditation cushion can be used to shed light on interpretive conundrums that have stumped readers of *The Cloud* for centuries. And conversely, instructions offered in *The Cloud*, once they are made intelligible in the light of practice, can be used as a yardstick to clarify and evaluate the still-developing body of Centering Prayer teaching, giving more forceful validation to instructions that are correct but challenging, and a yardstick for realignment when understanding is wandering off course.

The Cloud *at a Glance*

The Cloud of Unknowing is one of the great spiritual classics of medieval Christian mysticism. Most scholars agree that it was the work of an anonymous fourteenth-century English monastic, who some years later also contributed a second body of teachings known as *The Book of Privy Counsel.*[3] Like Rilke's *Letters to a Young Poet* five centuries later, it takes the form of a personal teaching offered by an older, more experienced monk to a younger one progressing along the path. Both of these parameters are important to keep in mind. *The Cloud* was not originally intended as a general spiritual manual, but as a customized instruction for a specific recipient whose heart the older monk already knew well. And these instructions are clearly not intended for a beginner, but for one who has already been well formed in the basic devotional and ethical aspects of the Christian path and is aspiring to the next level, which the author names "the contemplative."

Why is the author anonymous? This question has fueled speculation for centuries, leading to all sorts of conjectures, including that the author was a woman. But I think the most obvious explanation (aside from the fact that it was originally intended as a private communication) is simply that the era was a spiritually dangerous one. By 1329 the Roman Church had already condemned the mystical teachings of Meister Eckhart as the first cracks in the dike of the Roman Catholic theological monolith began to open. In Oxford, John Wycliffe was already agitating for a vernacular version of the Bible, and by the end of the century that version would in fact exist and be placed in the hands of laypeople by Wycliffe's followers, the Lollards: the headwaters of an insurrection that would erupt full-blown a little over a century later as the Protestant Reformation. It's clear, moreover, that our anonymous author is advocating some very dicey theological propositions: for starters, that "in this dark contemplation of the substance of your being . . . you are one with God"[4] or that "a naked intent direct to God is sufficient without anything else" (7-6). That sort of thinking could definitely get one burned at the stake!

As to the persistent speculation that the author is a woman, I have to say that much as I'd like to, I do not personally believe this is so. A simple fact-check reveals that being a woman posed no intrinsic obstacle to authorship, as demonstrated by *The Cloud* author's close contemporary, Dame Julian of Norwich, whose celebrated *Showings* are a cornerstone of the Western mystical tradition.[5] Much more personally persuasive, however, is that I experience the author's overall energy and imagery as intrinsically male. To take just one example (and there are many), if you return to that *Cloud* 7 passage already cited at the beginning of this chapter and read on into the next paragraph, you'll find the author advising: "This word shall be your shield and spear whether you ride in peace or war, and with that word you shall beat upon the cloud of unknowing and will strike down thoughts of every kind" (7-8). Even at the risk of gender stereotyping, unless our author is an early British Joan of Arc, I simply can't hear this as a woman's way of speaking! In contrast to Dame Julian with her hazelnut in hand, this author consistently draws his metaphoric stock from archery (5-2), jousting, and an overall backdrop of spiritual combat requiring strength and mettle. These are the qualities that give *The Cloud* its signature vibrancy, but the author who comes bursting off the page is, to my mind at least, unmistakably male.

The Translations

Over and above its spiritual significance, *The Cloud of Unknowing* is also of primary significance in the history of English literature, for it is among the very first spiritual treatises written in vernacular English. In fact, I first came to know this text as a graduate student in medieval literature, and my Early English Text Society version still sits on my bookshelf alongside a spate of modern translations as my court of final appeal. The work is written in Middle English, a brand-new language at the time, only just emerging out of its three main tributaries: Latin, Anglo Saxon, and French. *The Cloud* is roughly contemporaneous with Chaucer's *Canterbury Tales,* and the *Tales* indeed give wonderful insight into the rough-and-tumble spiritual times into which *The Cloud* was born. Just like Chaucer's, the language is earthy, picturesque, and filled with energy. There's a vibrancy to it—even a subtle humor—that is unfortunately largely lost in translation.

It's important, therefore, to realize that all the versions of *The Cloud* you'll probably be using are exactly that—translations. So the general rule when dealing with translations applies: get as many as you can and lay them out against each other as checks and balances. All translation is an art more than a science, and every translator's implicit assumptions ultimately bleed through.

The majority of my readers here, I suspect, will be most familiar with the William Johnston edition.[6] This is the version that William Meninger himself now prefers (though it was not yet in existence when he developed his prototypic method of

Centering Prayer), and it continues to hold pride of place in Trappist monastic circles, and thus, by extension, in Contemplative Outreach circles.

I have to admit, however, that I have significant reservations about the Johnston edition. Johnston translates through a heavy theological visor, and where *The Cloud* chafes up against it, he is not hesitant about introducing editorial "corrections" that are at best a misinterpretation and at worst an outright distortion of the original text. I have found numerous passages where words and even whole concepts were interpolated, making it very difficult to disentangle the text itself from the filter through which it is being viewed, and I will comment on some of these in due course. If you use the Johnston edition, it will be hard for you to see some of the points I will be making in my presentation: they are simply not there in the translation.

My own preferred edition continues to be Ira Progoff's (Delta Books, 1957). As a well-known depth psychologist and creator of the hugely popular Intensive Journal method, Progoff is precociously attuned to this work as a pioneering effort in the phenomenology of consciousness, and he translates with that acuity in mind. And as a secular psychologist, he simply end-runs all that theological overlay that so encumbers the Johnston edition. Progoff, too, must be monitored for the occasional temptation to overpsychologize or read in nuances that are not actually there in the text, but on the whole his translation weighs in well for accuracy, and his intuitive grasp of where this author is headed is superb.

A welcome newcomer to the field is Carmen Acevedo Butcher's sparkling, "relaxed fit" translation.[7] Like myself, Butcher approaches *The Cloud* from a background in medieval literature; she was for many years a professor of English at Shorter College, in Rome, Georgia. And no doubt our anonymous medieval author would be astonished to learn that his fourteenth-century spiritual treatise won the Georgia state literary award for 2010! When I first came upon this edition, the translation was so lively and contemporary that I assumed the author was taking huge liberties with the text—but no, her translation is actually closer to the original than many of the others so far mentioned. For newcomers to Christian mystical literature, I recommend this book hands down for its sheer immediacy—almost as if "Anonymous" (as Butcher cheekily addresses him) is sitting right there in the room with you—and for its fabulous way of conveying the energy of the medieval original. But Progoff slightly edges her out in the phenomenology department, and since that is my own major interest in *The Cloud,* I find myself eventually gravitating back to my well-thumbed Progoff version.

Whatever version is your present comfort zone, I strongly encourage you to reach out and make the acquaintance of another one. We need all the angles of approach available, all windows of insight wide open, as we begin this journey into what I hope to demonstrate for you about *The Cloud:* that rather than being a traditional specimen of Christian love mysticism, it is actually a groundbreaking phenomenological study, the first treatise ever written in the West that attempts to describe the transition to nondual consciousness understood *as a mode of perception, not a state of mystical union.* And as we shall see shortly, the touchstone to this transition, for this author, is an entirely new way of configuring attention.

CHAPTER 8

Objectless Awareness

What are you actually *doing* during a period of Centering Prayer? "Consenting to the presence and action of God," certainly. "Preparing the faculties to receive the gift of contemplation," yes, most likely.[1] But what are the actual mechanics of the process? Well, as the guidelines make clear, "When engaged with your thoughts, return ever-so-gently to the sacred word." So whatever else may be going on at the spiritual level, what you are actually doing is disengaging from your thoughts. Sometimes virtually nonstop. Again and again during that twenty-minute prayer period you find yourself releasing your attention from a thought it has managed to get tangled up in and returning it to a more spacious configuration.

Now, a thought, in Centering Prayer terminology, is anything that draws your attention to a focal point. It can be an inspiration. It can be a memory. It can be a sudden rush of emotion, or the brilliant final line of the sermon you're preparing for next Sunday. It can also, equally well, be an itch on your nose or the buzz of that damned fluorescent light overhead. If it draws your attention to the degree that you start engaging with it, it's a thought. And in Centering Prayer the marching orders are to let all thoughts go.

Why? The usual explanations given here have to do with "making yourself empty so that you can be filled with God," or reminders that a cluttered, preoccupied mind is hardly likely to be fully present—true enough. In my own teaching I prefer to come at it from a slightly different angle. Over the years I have gently but firmly insisted that one does not release a thought in order to achieve some desired result; the releasing itself is the full meaning of the prayer. I have attempted to explain this theologically on the basis of kenosis, or "letting go," which Saint Paul specifies (in his famous hymn of Philippians 2:6–11) as the very essence of "putting on the mind of Christ." Each time you manage to disengage from a thought, you are doing so in solidarity with Jesus's own kenotic stance, in the process patterning that stance more and more deeply into your being until it eventually becomes your default response to all life's situations.

I also need to emphasize yet one more time that you do not disengage from a thought *by replacing it with the sacred word*—at least insofar as that instruction is heard as *focusing* on the sacred word. This misimpression is still prevalent among many practitioners of Centering Prayer—and in the early attempts to present the method of Centering Prayer there was indeed some lack of clarity around this point. But you can see how using the word as a replacement focal point for your attention would essentially turn it into a mantra, and in the Thomas Keating version of Centering Prayer the sacred word is emphatically *not* a mantra, merely "a placeholder for your intention." The idea is not to stare at it, but merely to let it be the wiper blade that sweeps the windshield clean. While this distinction may at first seem to be maddeningly nuanced, you'll see shortly that there's a lot riding on it.

Have you ever watched really closely what happens when you release a thought? Yes, in most cases more thoughts come rushing back in. But notice how there is a slight gap between them; if only for a nanosecond, there occurs a moment when you are present and alert, but in which your attention is focused on no particular thing. You are briefly in a state of *objectless awareness.*

This fleeting taste, in the gap between the thoughts, of a whole different bandwidth of consciousness is commented on extensively in the Eastern meditation traditions and in some small pockets of inner work in the Western esoteric tradition, but the vast mainstream of Christian theological and devotional tradition goes flying right through it like a stop sign, never even noticing it's there. If you *do* notice it's there, however, and begin to learn how to work with it, it will open up a whole new approach not only to your own spiritual evolution but also to some of those more formidable masterpieces of our own Western spiritual tradition, *The Cloud of Unknowing* prominently included.

Attention, as we normally understand it here in the West, is implicitly an energy connecting subject to object: "I pay attention to my driving." "I pay attention to the lecture." "I put my attention on my breathing." If we have good powers of attention, we can place our attention on any object we so choose and hold it there voluntarily, regardless of whether that object is inherently interesting or not. If not, our attention is "grabbed" involuntarily and weathercocks in the direction of each new passing stimulus (that state the Buddhists call "monkey mind"). But whether our attention is strong or weak, it is expected to fall on an object. When I say, "Pay attention," people will immediately respond, "To what?" For how can you pay attention if there's no "what" to pay attention to?

But there is also a different possible configuration for the attention, in which it does not flow in a straight line linking subject to object, but can rather hold a certain tensile strength as a three-dimensional field of awareness. As I have previously noted, the best way I can describe it is through that beautiful metaphor from Rumi, already introduced in chapter 4: "quivering like a drop of mercury."

If you can still recall mercury from the time before ecological concerns drove it out of widespread household use, you'll remember the curious way it behaves when you remove it from its container and let it organize itself on a flat surface. It can either act like a liquid and spread out in a puddle, or it can hold its own shape as a drop, rolling about like a Weeble. Your attention is much like that. In its "liquid" form it connects subject to object. In its solid, "Weeble" form, it is a tensile field of vibratory awareness, within which you can be conscious of the whole without having to split the field into the usual subject/object polarity. It is actually a higher energetic state. The Tibetan Buddhists call it *rigpa:* "pure awareness."

And I have come to suspect that the contemplative masters of our own Christian lineage were also well aware of this state and that this is actually what is intended by the word "vigilance" in the Eastern Orthodox tradition and "recollection" in the West. It doesn't mean thinking deeply about something, recalling it. Rather, it means that *you yourself* are gathered—"re-collected"—within that deeper inner attentiveness whose much more powerful energetic vibrancy allows a different mode of perception to unfold. In the nanosecond between the cessation of one thought and the arising of the next, there is a moment of pure consciousness where subject and object poles drop out and you're simply *there*. For a nanosecond, there's no "you" and no God. No experience and no experiencer. There's simply a direct, undivided, sensate awareness of a single, unified field of being perceived from a far deeper place of aliveness. And what is first tasted in a nanosecond can indeed become a stable and integrated state.

Now I would ask you keep that possibility in the backdrop of your mind as we return now for a second look at Thomas Keating's very challenging—but absolutely correct—teaching about the handling of thoughts during prayer time. This is of course one of the four cornerstone lectures in the Centering Prayer introductory workshop, but it so goes against the grain of everything we have been taught to believe about the spiritual life that nearly everybody struggles against it mightily, sometimes for years. In this teaching, you recall from those introductory workshops, Keating specifies five kinds of thoughts that can make a play for your attention during the time of Centering Prayer ("woolgathering" or random thoughts, "attractive" thoughts, insights and illuminations, self-reflection, and thoughts from the unconscious). It is the third set that concerns us here.

Insights and illuminations, as defined by Keating, are sudden inspirations and revelations that appear out of nowhere once a Centering Prayer period is well underway and the surface distractions have settled down. Suddenly a flash of understanding lights up the night sky of your mind: a new psychological insight, a creative inspiration, a vision, or even the overwhelming desire to pray for everyone then and there. This inspiration is always appropriately "spiritual" in content, sometimes even bearing the distinct impression of an angelic visitation. It nearly always has a dreamy or mirage-like quality to it. And it infallibly carries the same message: "Put the Centering Prayer on hold and pay attention to this stunning new bit of content!"

And the instructions under the circumstances? Always the same four R's: "Resist no thought, retain no thought, react to no thought, return ever so gently to the sacred word."

Ouch!

We come by this struggle honestly. We've been raised in a Judeo-Christian religious culture in which we're accustomed to thinking of silence and solitude as the conditions par excellence for receiving divine messages. From Moses in the wilderness with his burning bush to Elijah and his "still small voice," to John the Baptist and Jesus himself departing periodically into the desert in order to receive their divine marching orders, we're well habituated to thinking of silence as simply the formal preliminary to receiving content. This already established proclivity has been reinforced still more strongly by contemporary metaphors emerging out of depth psychology in which the unconscious becomes the inner wilderness and meditation a primary tool for psychological uncovering.[2]

In fact, I once had an Anglican abbot, the founder of a very serious-minded and traditional contemplative order, challenge me on precisely this point. "If God is going to go to all the trouble to send me a message during the time of my prayer, then I am certainly going to have the courtesy to listen to him!" That is the conventional wisdom for sure. But it is not the wisdom of Centering Prayer.

The turning point in my own understanding of this doggedly counterintuitive point came about fifteen years ago during a five-day Centering Prayer intensive retreat I was leading at the Vancouver School of Theology. We were almost exactly at the midpoint of the retreat—during the second Centering Prayer period in the second triple sit on the third day—when sitting there on my meditation cushion, I was indeed visited by what seemed to be the brass ring of all insights and illuminations. (Of course, it goes with the turf that I now have not even the faintest recollection of what it might have been about.) I was reaching out to grab it when suddenly, in an instant of unequivocal knowing, I realized that if I took the bait, I would be instantly jerked back to the surface of my mind, into a bandwidth of consciousness that was familiar, dull, and infinitely less alive than the vibrant aliveness going on here at the depths. Keating uses the analogy of switching a TV screen from full color back to black-and-white; it was indeed like that. With overpowering clarity I knew that the vibrancy of the communion palpably going on in my depths depended on maintaining my attention in that objectless awareness mode, "quivering like a drop of mercury." Even the most glorious spiritual content would only result in downgrading the vibration of my attentiveness to its ordinary level.

If you've ever had a similar experience, you'll recognize firsthand what Keating is talking about in this teaching and appreciate its sheer spiritual audacity. He is not going for the brass ring here; he is going for the gold, and once you actually taste it, it will shift the center of your practice as it shifted mine. Those siren calls from the surface simply lose their appeal as you slowly awaken to the astounding possibility that *all that content you're being tempted with is being dangled before a "you" that doesn't really exist anyway*!

What do I mean here? Essentially this: that the subject-object configuration of your attention generates a corresponding sense of selfhood. Through the lens of our usual attentional pattern, who "I" am feels like a mysterious interiority at the subject pole flowing out to a set of concrete attributes at the object pole. These are the defining characteristics that collectively confer on each one of us our unique identity by differentiating us from everybody else. And our quest for "our true self" flows back and forth on that attentional bridge like a hamster on a treadmill. As we fervently struggle to "realize" ourselves by replacing false definitions of ourselves with relatively more correct ones, to meet the question "Who am I?" with a set of finite attributes, we do not yet notice that we are trapped within the givens of the perceptual program we are running. Hunting for the true self within this hall of mirrors is like questing for the proverbial mythical unicorn: it can only yield a mirage.

Mirages can indeed be compelling. I have told the story many times now of sitting one evening, just at sunset, in a small twin-engine commercial airplane about to take off into a decidedly foggy and low-visibility night. As the prop began to turn, suddenly a spotlight came on at the gate and shone directly through the now rapidly turning blades. From where I was sitting, it looked like a golden ball sitting there on the wing, so real that I could put my hand out and touch it. But the golden ball was of course only a mirage, created by light passing through a turning propeller.

In the same way, I would propose that this "self" we're so completely caught up in 90 percent of our waking time is a mirage, a ray of light passing through a turning propeller. This "I" I am trying so hard to purify, manage, and "realize"—this chief protagonist of my spiritual journey, this lifetime project I've somehow taken on, to improve it, find a truer version of it, dismantle its false self and claim its true self, discover its enneagram type or its spiritual vocation, march it through the spiritual exercises or take down its secret soul messages through dream analysis—*this* self doesn't really exist! It is simply the inevitable byproduct of attention flowing in the subject/object configuration, which creates the illusion of solidity in the first place. That golden ball sitting on the plane wing is not really there.

In those deeper waters of Centering Prayer—in those nanoseconds (at first) between the thoughts, when your attention is not running out ahead to grab the next object to alight upon, you taste those first precious drops of an entirely different quality of selfhood. As the author of *The Cloud of Unknowing* puts it, you "pay attention not to what you are, but to *that* you are."[3] With all due respect to our author, I might emend that slightly to say you pay attention *from* what you are: from that deeper pool of recollected selfhood. There is a deeper current of living awareness, a deeper and more intimate sense of belonging, which flows beneath the surface waters of your being and grows stronger and steadier as your attention is able to maintain itself as a unified field of objectless awareness.

At first it feels like a place you go to—"my inner well-spring"—and your ego-self comes with its bucket to fill itself up. But that is merely because attention is still weak. Objectless awareness is a higher vibrational state; it requires energy to hold yourself there. But there is a learning curve here, and the system gradually acclimates. The closest analogy I can come up with here is in studying a foreign language. Let's say you're learning Spanish. For the first several months, when you hear a phrase in Spanish, you first mentally translate it into English to make sense of it; then you translate it back into Spanish to respond. But there comes a time in your mastery of the language when the translation step finally drops out; you hear directly in Spanish and respond directly in Spanish. The contemplative life is like that as well.

For a while, yes, our ego-self does indeed appear to be the stable operator. We draw our water from the spiritual well and then bring it home to translate into all the benefits it confers on our daily lives. From there we translate our thanks back to God in the form of wordless or spoken prayer. But there comes a time when the ego translator drops out, and we are simply *there*, hearing and responding directly in the native language of being. There is oneness. And that is fundamentally what is meant by nondual consciousness. Then this "inner wellspring" is no longer a place you go to; it's a place you *come from*. It's a whole new structure of consciousness that can perceive without first splitting the field.

From this perspective, it's a bit disheartening to acknowledge that the vast bulk of our Christian spiritual literature, devotional experience, mysticism, and spiritual practices operates solidly within the field of separated or "translator" consciousness. Even our highest vision of spiritual attainment—the unitive state—is typically described in affective metaphors (such as mystical marriage), leading one to believe that what goes on there is an ecstatic consummation of "my" soul in God, the highest possible state of beatific splendor and grace.

But nondual consciousness is not a state. It's not a mystical experience. It is not necessarily blissful. You can't attain it. You can't come back from it transformed because there is no "you" left to be transformed. It is not an intensification of union. It is simply a quiet erasing of the line that divided the field in the first place.

I know that is a tough bite for Western minds to swallow. We so want to have our cake and eat it too—to be transformed and live to tell the tale! But beneath all the surface chatter there is a wholly different sphere of awareness, a different sphere of selfhood, a different sense of God's presence, a different way of relating to our human tasks that doesn't go through the translating mechanism of the separated self having experiences of oneness. We don't hear a lot of people talking about it in Christianity. Meister Eckhart is clearly talking about it. In our own times, Bernadette Roberts is talking about it. And I believe *The Cloud of Unknowing* is also talking about it, but in ways we have barely begun to appreciate.

CHAPTER 9

Nothing but God (Cloud 3)

When I first came upon this chapter as a young spiritual seeker many decades ago, I have to confess that it stopped me dead in my tracks. I remember my sinking feeling as I stared at the words leaping out at me from the page: "Seek God and none of his created things";[1] "Think of nothing but God himself";[2] "Forget all the beings whom God created and all their works."[3]

What was a budding young contemplative to do? Of course I took the instruction here literally: to "seek God Himself and none of His created things." I thought that meant I was to spend every moment of my time thinking about God, chasing all other thoughts away. Then, a couple of chapters later, when I read, "But of God no man can think," I was totally confused!

I suspect I am not the only Christian contemplative to have struggled hard with the perplexing and sometimes contradictory demands of *The Cloud of Unknowing*. The mystery begins to resolve itself, however, when you see that the author is really talking about the *configuration* of your attention, not the *object* of your attention. Just as in Centering Prayer, anything that brings your attention to a focal point is a "thought," and a thought blocks objectless awareness, the only mode in which God can be accessed or "known." Our author, then, is asking us to withdraw our attention from all external objects not because these objects are in themselves unworthy of respect, but because attention in the subject/object configuration can never ultimately reach its goal of participative union with God.

It took me decades to figure this out, and when I did, it was directly through the time logged on the meditation cushion in Centering Payer. But at long last, the author's meaning came clear. It's a close parallel to what happens to our visual field when we shift from cones to rods: from the sharp focus of dayseeing to the peripheral perception of "night vision." When our author asks us to "do whatever will help you forget all the beings whom God has created and all their works," he's not advocating hard-heartedness, but merely recommending that we move beyond object-focused prayer (even worthy objects!). In the classic language of the Christian contemplative tradition, we are practicing moving from a *cataphatic* way of knowing (i.e., with an object-focused awareness) to an *apophatic,* or "formless" (i.e., objectless) awareness, emanating from a deeper capacity of the human soul in God.

The author's pet metaphor for this field (or mode) of objectless awareness is *the cloud of unknowing.* And once you crack the code here, everything else in his teaching begins to fall into line.

Chapters 3, 5, 6, and 7 furnish the essential building blocks of his presentation here, and hence of my argument. So I propose now to have a close look at these chapters, pretty much paragraph by paragraph, so that you can see for yourself what I'm getting at. While my interpretation may at first seem unlikely, it's actually there in the text—*if* you're dealing with the actual text, that is! So what you'll be reading from in these next few chapters, unless otherwise specifically noted, is my own raw (i.e., as close to literal as possible) translation of the Middle English from the original Early English Text Society

Edition.[4] The only thing I've changed are the *thees* and *thous,* a few archaic verb endings, and a *very* few words that no longer exist in modern English, for which I've substituted the most direct modern English equivalent. Admittedly, the final result is not nearly as punchy as Carmen Acevedo Butcher's, but it does let you have a look at the "straight-up" text as free as possible from interpretive innovations. And since I suspect the majority of readers will have encountered the text only through these varying interpretive lenses, I thought it might be useful for a variety of reasons to put the original version into wider circulation.

A Meek Stirring of Love

> Lift up your heart unto God with a meek stirring of love, and intend by that himself and none of his goods. And to that end, be loath to think on anything else but on himself, so that nothing works in your mind or in your will but only himself. And to do that in yourself is to forget all the creatures that ever God made and their works so that your thoughts and your desires are not directed or stretched to any of them, either in general or in specific. But let them be, and take no notice of them. (3-1)

This first paragraph introduces the basic idea already alluded to, suggesting that in contemplation the usual configuration of attention must be suspended, so that "nothing works in your mind or your will." Our author identifies this other pathway of cognition as residing in the heart and describes its modality by the word "love." But as we shall see shortly, what he has in mind by love is nothing like what most of us would intend by that term.

Admittedly, the statement "be loath to think on anything

but Himself" continues to be problematic even in the most literal rendition. It was apparently so for our author as well, for three chapters later he will correct himself on this point and concede, "Of God no man can think." The culprit here is really the word "think." Our author is struggling to find a word that means "to be conscious of," but the word "think" is clearly not the right candidate for the job, tying him right back into what he actually sees as the major impediment to the state of conscious awareness he's trying to describe.

If we can move beyond specific words to the more general context clues, the picture begins to fill in. While "thinking on nothing else but God" will still bear some clarification (coming in *Cloud* 6), the overall drift is already clear that the goal is to restrain the attention from running out to specific objects and to remain recollected at some deeper point within. "Creatures"—in this case and consistently throughout *The Cloud*—*are specific focal points* for the attention, and just as in Centering Prayer, the instruction is to "let them be" (i.e., "resist no thought"), *but not to focus on them or to allow your desire to be hooked by them* ("retain no thought"). He is trying to say "Don't let your consciousness divide; don't let your attentional field split into subject and object"—a message that by this point in our discussion is at least recognizable once seen in that light.

A small but not insignificant point: note that in the original Middle English the actual wording of that first instruction is to "mene" God, which is neither quite "seek" God as in Progoff or "focus on" God as in Butcher. It comes closest to "intend" God and does not necessarily imply an object or focal point for the faculties so much as that deeper underlying intentionality that our author will refer to throughout the text as a "naked intent to God." And the phrase "mene himself and none of his goodes" does not necessarily mean that these goods are neces- sarily *things*. According to long-standing spiritual tradition, they can also be consolations, visions, "insights and illuminations," fantasies, ecstatic states—anything that goes into comprising spiritual wealth, with its accompanying sense of privilege and possessiveness.

The Most Pleasing Soul Work

> This is the work of the soul that most pleases God. All saints and angels have joy in this work and hasten to help it with all their might. All the fiends are angry when you do it and will try to thwart it in every way they can. All men living on earth are wonderfully helped by this work in ways you know not. Yes, the souls in purgatory are eased of their pain by virtue of this work. And you yourself are cleansed and made virtuous by no other work as much as this. And yet it is the lightest work of all, and the most speedily accomplished if one is helped with the grace of a perceptible desire. Otherwise it is hard and a wonder that you can do it. (3-2)

This paragraph may at first read like quite the hype job for the contemplative life. It turns out, however, that these claims rest on a very ancient and solid lineage of Christian spiritual teaching that insists that the demons (whether construed as external forces or internal ones) can only reach you through *the power of your imagination*—or in other words, when you allow your attention to "close" on an object of your own mental creation. When you seize on a thought or commentary (*logismoi*, as the fourth-century teacher Evagrius called them) as it flashes across your mental screen and clamors for your attention, then you are hooked. If you don't grab it, it can't grab you.

This is of course exactly the opposite of what you'll some-times hear in the recent fundamentalist rhetoric that "the devil will get you if you make your mind a blank," used to scare people away from the practice of meditation. Aside from the fact that objectless awareness is a very, very far cry from "making your mind a blank," this recent, post-Freudian scare tactic[5] flies in the face of the traditional Christian teaching that it is only when you take the bait and engage with an object of your imagination that the passions are engaged and turmoil ensues.

In fact, it is precisely because they had not yet learned this vital lesson, argued the eleventh-century spiritual master Simeon the New Theologian (whom we have already met up with in part two of this book), that would-be desert hermits would sometimes get into trouble, attempting solitude without having first mastered their own minds. If for most of his previous prayer life,

> a man stands at prayer and, raising his hands, his eyes and his mind to heaven, keeps in mind divine thoughts, imagines celestial blessings, hierarchies of angels and dwellings of the saints, assembles briefly in his mind all he has learned from the Holy Scriptures and ponders over all this while at prayer, gazing up to heaven, and thus inciting his soul to longing and love of God, at times even shedding tears and weeping,

then the strong reliance on the imagination, together with the high excitation of the emotions, is ultimately self-delusional and can become addictive, leading him to depend on lights, sweet scents, and "other like phenomena" as evidence of the presence of God. "If then such a man give himself up to silence," Simeon adds bluntly, "he can scarcely avoid going out of his mind."[6]

The only safe route, Simeon counsels, is through developing a strict mental equanimity in which the thoughts do not affix themselves to the bait dangled by the imagination. As you recall, he calls this capacity "attention of the heart." It is the essence of his much preferred "third method of attention and prayer." It is also the essence of the method of Centering Prayer.

As to the angels loving this "work of the soul," well, it's obvious, when you come to think about it, that the root of all contentiousness, misery, warfare, and evil is *the mind in the identified position*—firmly and passionately wrapped around its fixation of choice. This can be an ideal, a self-image, a cause to be won, a wrong to be righted; in the end it winds up looking pretty much the same. I would dare to wager that no misery has ever been launched onto the planet with the attention *not* in this configuration. But as we gain the capacity to "let the thoughts be," holding the field of presence in a different way, a new sort of energy begins to emerge, of a markedly higher luminosity and range. Within this field of concentrated "spiritual generativity" (as contemporary Carmelite Constance Fitzgerald calls it),[7] we discover that not only are we connected to all other such fields on this earth plane, but it is indeed possible to give and receive assistance from other realms of existence as well—even "those souls in purgatory," as our author rightly observes. Far from a hype job on the contemplative life, he is merely stating an objective truth about the power of attention held in an undivided perceptual field.

Before leaving this section, it is worth noting how here, as consistently throughout *The Cloud,* our author refers to this contemplative engagement as a "work." We are well before the era of John of the Cross and those ensuing spiritual dichotomies of "acquired" versus "infused" grace.[8] In *The Cloud's* version, the aspiring contemplative is expected to participate actively in the task of "cleansing the lens of perception" through a committed engagement with practices being laid out, the fundamental aim of which, in Progoff's perceptive appraisal, "is to break through the bonds that attach the individual to the world of his senses and separate him from his eternal nature."[9]

Entering the Cloud

> Do not let up, therefore, but work in this way till you feel the desire. For at the beginning when you do this, you will find only a darkness, and, as it were, a cloud of unknowing—you know not what—except that you feel in your will a naked intent unto God. No matter what you do, this cloud and this darkness are between you and your God and block you, so that you may not see him clearly by the light of understanding in your reason, nor may you feel him in sweetness of love in your affection. And therefore prepare yourself to abide in this darkness as long you may, evermore crying out after him that you love. For if ever you shall feel him or see him as it may be here, it behooves you always to be in this cloud and this darkness. And if you will work industriously as I bid you, I trust in his mercy that you shall arrive there. (3-3)

Our chapter opened, as you recall, with the author's celebrated instruction to "lift up your heart with a meek stirring of love." In this final paragraph he returns to the subject of love, but in such a way as to throw a major monkey wrench into our usual understanding of this term.

It's tempting to think that *The Cloud of Unknowing* is simply asking us to "get out of our heads and into our hearts," and as we've seen, it has often been interpreted that way, as a classic example of Christian affective mysticism. But those who would believe that the love he is talking about here is affectivity (understood as the emotional qualities of feeling and desire) must then somehow explain away his specific stipulation that you cannot see God either by the light of your reason *nor by the sweetness of your love in your affection.*

And then our author layers on yet another paradox: although it takes a strong desire to do this contemplative "work," you must work until you feel the desire! Clearly the chief operative here cannot possibly be *emotional desire,* as is the case in classic affective mysticism. No, it is, as he says, simply a "naked intent" carried at some deeper level of your being. Thomas Keating is quite correct in his assessment that the quality our author is talking about comes closer to will than to the emotion of love, but we must be careful not to equate it with the *faculty* of will as in classic scholastic theology—and even less with willpower. It is rather some capacity of knowingness and willingness emanating from a place far deeper within us that won't let us *not* do the work, whether we like it or not. This "love" our author has in mind is of a different order altogether; it rises on the other side of the cataphatic/apophatic watershed.

In this final paragraph the author also introduces his fundamental metaphor, the "cloude of unknowing" in its original Middle English rendition. Like virtually all his metaphors, this one is allusive, showing forth different facets of itself under different lights. The most immediate meaning here is that the cloud represents an overriding or blocking of our normal "faculties" (again in the scholastic sense of the term)—in this case, the faculties of reason and emotion.

The faculties are fundamentally *avenues of perception,* and whether you are talking about reason, emotion, memory, or will (the big four), the bottom line is that they all work with the attention in the subject/object configuration. That's how cataphatic perception works. They presuppose a fundamental subject, "I," making use of one of those modalities to connect with the intended object—in this case, God.

Our author is suggesting that when we move into this new "work," our former mode of perception goes dark. It's not that God is absent or you are absent; it's merely that the cloud is *between* you and God (which, as Ira Progoff insightfully notes, is a term that implies connection as well as separation). The cloud—fuzzy, diffuse, sheltering, enveloping—will be the new modus operandi in which you will come to apprehend the divine presence. And you have to admit, it's a pretty apt metaphor for this new, soft-edged mode of perception, this kind of spiritual night vision that allows you to see by not staring directly at the object ahead. Both functionally and metaphorically the "cloud of unknowing" is a picturesque way to evoke the quality of objectless awareness.

CHAPTER 10

The Heart of the Cloud
(Cloud 5 and 6)

As I have mentioned already, it is not my intention here to offer a complete commentary on *The Cloud of Unknowing*. That is beyond the scope of this present book, but even more important, it is tangential to my real purpose here, which is to trace the thread of objectless awareness as it weaves its way beneath the surface of metaphor in this remarkably precocious medieval exploration of the approach route to nondual consciousness. Because that is my aim, I will reluctantly pass over *Cloud* 4, which takes us a bit off topic (even though it is one of my personal favorites, and I'll return to it briefly at the end of the book), and focus here on *Cloud* 5 and 6, which bring us right to the eye of the needle.

These two chapters are among the shortest in *The Cloud*—only five paragraphs between them—but they convey the gist of the teaching with a brilliant directness and force. If you can wrap your mind around what's going on here, the rest of *The Cloud* will begin to fall into place. In *Cloud* 5, our author's emphasis is on the withdrawal of attention from all external objects. In *Cloud* 6 he takes us a quantum leap further into his profound intuition of love not as affection, but as an entirely new mode of spiritual cognition.

Target Practice: Cloud 5

This brief chapter contains the key proof text confirming that our author's real concern in this teaching is with the *configuration of our attention*. As he lays out his guidelines for the "work" of contemplation, he is actually exploring *the phenomenology of objectless awareness*.

THE CLOUD OF FORGETTING

And if ever you shall come to this cloud and live and work therein as I bid you, it behooves you—since this cloud of unknowing is above you, between you and your God—straightaway to put a cloud of forgetting beneath you, between you and all the creatures that have ever been made. You might think, perhaps, that you are very far away from God because this cloud of unknowing is between you and your God, but certainly, as it can be well imagined, you are much farther from him when you have no cloud of forgetting between you and all the creatures that ever have been made. As often as I say, "All the creatures that have ever been made," just so I mean not only the creatures themselves, but also all the works and the conditions of these same creatures. I make exception here for not a single creature, whether they be bodily creatures or spiritual ones, nor a single condition or work of any creature, whether they be good or evil. But in short, all should be hidden under the cloud of forgetting in this case. (5-1)

Here our author restates his initial premise from *Cloud* 3, that in order to enter this new perceptual terrain, it is necessary first to withdraw our attention from all "creatures"—that is, all specific objects of attention. He picturesquely suggests that we wrap them up in a "cloud of forgetting." For practitioners of Centering Prayer, this "companion" cloud is readily grasped, probably far more so that the cloud of unknowing itself. It corresponds to that slight movement of the will—"refocusing the camera lens of our intention," as Thomas Keating puts it—that occurs when we recognize that we're engaged with a thought and promptly let it go. Spaciousness returns as we settle ourselves back down within the cloud of unknowing. Even though our *subjective* experience of this fuzzy, diffuse awareness may feel like a long, long ways from God, our author reassures us that we are actually a lot closer to our destination when we are hunkered down within the cloud than when our attention is constantly being pulled outward toward specific focal points, no matter how worthy.

THE ARCHER AND HIS TARGET

> For although it may be quite profitable to think some-times of certain conditions and deeds of some certain special creatures, nevertheless, yet in this work it profits little or nothing. This is because caring or thinking of any creature that ever God made, or of any of their other deeds is a kind of spiritual light; for the eye of your soul is opened on it and even fixed thereupon, just as the eye of an archer is upon the target he is shooting at. And one thing I will tell you: that any thing that you think about is above you for a time, and between you and your God. And to just such a degree you are farther from God if you are concerned about anything else but God. (5-2)

In this paragraph he develops his crucial point by means of the metaphor of the archer aiming at a target. Just as the target completely captures the archer's attention, so any thought or memory becomes a target for "the eye of your soul" as your attention is completely captured by it. In this vividly kines-thetic image, the author demonstrates his intuitive grasp of the dynamics of attention and his keen awareness of the difference between attention bound to a mental object and *free attention*—that is, attention flowing as an innate property of consciousness itself. While he doesn't use the term "object-less awareness," he clearly recognizes the state and offers his metaphor of the cloud of unknowing as a remarkably close fourteenth-century approximation.

Incidentally, you will miss this crucial teaching altogether if you're using the Johnston edition. Instead of what is actually written in the text, you will find this inscrutable paraphrase: "Thinking and remembering are forms of spiritual under-standing in which the eye of the spirit is opened and closed upon things as the eye of a marksman is on his target."[1]

THE NAKED BEING OF GOD

Yes, and if it be courteous and appropriate to say so, in this work it profits little or nothing to think on the kindness and worthiness of God, nor on our Lady, nor on the saints and angels in heaven, nor even on the joys of heaven: that is, with a special attentiveness [literally, "beholding"] of them as if by that attentiveness to feed and increase your purpose. I believe it is not like that at all in this case and in this work. For although it is good to think upon the kindness of God and to love and praise him for this, yet it is far better to think upon the naked being of him and to love and praise him for him-self. (5-3)

Once you grasp that our author really *is* talking about the configuration of attention, then it becomes much more obvious why memory and all those other worthy objects of our spiritual attention—God, our Lady, the joys of heaven—"profit little or nothing in this work." For the work lies precisely in learning how to withdraw our attention from objects so that it can be gathered and magnetized at a far deeper level of spiritual attentiveness. From these depths of recollection, we can begin to come into resonance with God's "naked being," as the author expresses it, and "to love and praise Him for Himself."

"By Love but Not by Thought": Cloud 6

But now you ask me and say, "How shall I think on himself and what is he?" And to this I can only answer you, "I do not know." (6-1)

For you have brought me with this question into that same darkness and into that same cloud of unknowing that I wish you to be in yourself. For of all other creatures and their works—yea, and of the works of God himself—may a man through grace have full knowledge and can very well think on them, but of God himself no man can think. And therefore I choose to leave all those things that I can think upon and choose for my love that one thing on which I cannot think. By love he may be gotten and held, but not by thought. And therefore, although it may be good sometimes to think of the kindness and the worthiness of God in a particular way, and although it is a delight and a part of contemplation, nevertheless in this work it shall be cast down and covered with a cloud of forgetting. And you shall step above it resolutely but joyfully with a devout and pleasing stirring of love and try to pierce the darkness above you. And strike upon that thick cloud of unknowing with a sharp dart of longing love and do not leave whatever may befall. (6-2)

In this chapter our author fine-tunes his earlier instruction (the one that confused me so much as a first-time *Cloud* reader) that we should think only about God. Now he admits candidly, "Of God himself no man can think." The only way to make contact is through love. Whatever that may mean.

Typically we think of love as having something to do with emotions—with our feelings of affection. But if we assume that this is what our author has in mind, we quickly tumble into the sand trap of that old "head versus heart" dichotomy. We think the message here is that God cannot be accessed by mental/cognitive routes (and that much is indeed true!), but if we can fan our feelings of devotion to a sufficient ardor, God will indeed show up.

But already in *Cloud* 3 our author has warned us that God cannot be known by *either* of these routes: "You can neither see Him clearly with your reason in the light of understanding, nor can you feel Him with your affection in the sweetness of love." Whatever the author means by love, it is something of an entirely different order from our usual sense of devotion and affection. It is not a property of our cataphatic faculties (memory, reason, emotion, will), but of something that emerges from far deeper in the soul. (He often uses the word "naked" to point to it, as in "a naked intent to God," or "God's naked being.")

The poet Rilke once famously advised us to live the questions rather than seek for easy answers,[2] and to live the question "What does our author mean by love?" is one of the most profoundly illuminating ways of entering deeply into this work (both the work of understanding the book and the work of your own contemplative transformation). If you are patient, the meaning will gradually reveal itself, like pieces of a puzzle slowly filling in.

My own suspicion, informed by modern neuroscience as well as by my earlier studies on attention of the heart, is that by "love" he is really talking about *heart-centered cognition,* as opposed to the binary, linear, and analytical mode of cognition of the brain. And heart-centered cognition, neuroscientists are now telling us, is really a kind of "operating system," a way of organizing the perceptual field so that we perceive holographically (through electromagnetic resonance) rather than through the subject/object differentiation fundamental to brain-centered cognition. Heart-centered cognition is the foundational physiological prerequisite for the emergence of a stable nondual consciousness.

None of this was known back in the fourteenth century, of course. Even today, the perception is only beginning to arise that nondual perception is not about what you see, but *how* you see; it is not an "experience," but a whole new modality of perception. Against this backdrop, it is amazing to watch this anonymous mystic working intuitively toward a program of "retraining the brain" through withdrawing attention from objects (which reinforces mental cognition) and learning to gather it into a central reservoir of spiritual attentiveness, the necessary physiological prerequisite for brain/heart entrainment. By calling it "love," he is essentially saying, "It has to do with the heart." Don't look for it anywhere else.

STRIKE UPON THAT CLOUD?

The final instructions in this chapter are admittedly a bit of a scramble. Having just spent most of the last two chapters insisting that that cloud will always be there "between you and your God"—and that it in fact constitutes the normal mode of communication between the two of you for the duration of your earthly life—he is now inviting us to beat upon it and strike it down with a sharp dart of longing love. All of a sudden we are in warrior mode (and this is the primary passage on which I draw my inference that our anonymous author can only be male). My own take is that he has allowed his metaphor to run away with him a bit here. But then I am reminded of an extraordinary comment made by Thomas Merton in his correspondence with the Sufi mystic Abdul Aziz, which, I suspect, might shed some light on our author's paradoxical instructions here:

> My prayer tends very much toward what you call *fana* [annihilation in God]. There is in my heart this great thirst to recognize totally the nothingness of all that is not God. My prayer is then a kind of praise rising up out of the center of Nothing and Silence. If I am still present "myself," this I recognize as an obstacle about which I can do nothing unless He Himself removes the obstacle. If He wills, He can make the Nothingness into a total clarity. If He does not will, then the Nothingness seems itself to be an object and remains an obstacle. Such is my ordinary way of prayer, or meditation. It is not "thinking about" anything, but a direct seeking of the Face of the Invisible, who cannot be found unless we become lost in Him who is invisible.[3]

Like Merton, our medieval author seems to be affirming that the cloud can ultimately melt in moments of dazzling unity. But to seek these moments directly while still living within our usual small-self skin is merely to prolong our sojourn in the halls of mirrors of phenomenal experience. If we are to aspire to that undivided perceptual field that is for this author the essence of the contemplative work, then we must let the experiencing self go once and for all, and accept whatever may or may not ensue. That "naked intent direct to God" is deeper, ultimately, than even the most dazzling perception of clarity.

CHAPTER II

Jousting with Thoughts (Cloud 7)

This chapter is probably the most well known in the entire *Cloud of Unknowing* because it furnishes the direct source for Centering Prayer. It is here, in those pivotal sixth and seventh paragraphs, that Father William Meninger unearthed the building block that would become the cornerstone of Centering Prayer.

But this chapter contains another treasure as well, often overlooked as contemporary practitioners of Centering Prayer quickly flip through the first five paragraphs to arrive at their premier proof text. But here in these five paragraphs you'll find a dramatic dialogue between the seeker and a pesky thought intent on derailing him. The dialogue is in its own way hilarious. (I'd love to do a staged reading someday!) But even more so, it reveals an extremely subtle understanding of how taking the bait of an "attractive" thought dangled before you—even a pious or holy thought—can wind up scrambling the state of objectless awareness and cause you to wobble in your orbit and eventually tumble back into the field of ordinary consciousness. (As a fourteenth-century Christian, he doesn't use this metaphor, of course, but I think you'll see how accurately it captures the degradation of conscious attention he is in fact vividly describing here.) In toto, these five paragraphs provide the most powerful validation I've yet come across for Thomas Keating's famously challenging teaching on handling insights and illuminations during Centering Prayer time.

"Go Thou down Again!"

> And if any thought should arise and press constantly above you, between you and that darkness, and ask you, "What are you seeking and what would you have?" say that it is God that you would have: "Him I covet, him I seek, and nothing but him." And if he [i.e., the thought] asks you, "What is that God?" say that it is God that made you and bought you and has graciously called you to his love. "And in him," you are to say, "you have no skill!" And therefore say, "Go thou down again!" and tread him fast down with a stirring of love, even though he seems to you quite holy and seems as if he might help you in seeking God.
>
> It may be that he will bring to your mind a great many diverse and wonderful points about his kindness and say that he is so sweet and loving, so gracious and merciful. And if you hear him out, he likes nothing better, and he will jangle on and on until at last he brings you down [literally, "lower"] to the remembrance of his Passion. (7-1, 7-2a)

As "Mr. Thought" begins his seduction, note that the first bait dangled is simply the temptation to think *about* God, rather than resting in that darkness until your spiritual night vision begins to fill in. It's a well-engrained cataphatic habit to think about God during prayer time—to listen for messages or marvel at the divine qualities—and this clever saboteur "helpfully" furnishes the material to lure you back into cataphatic perception. Starting with what seems to be an innocent and even holy meditation upon God's noble qualities, he then hooks your emotions by dangling the bait of the Passion.

Once you've allowed your emotions to be so hooked, it's an easy step into an abyss of self-reflection with its accompanying inner turmoil.

That final phrase—"till he brings you down to the remembrance of His Passion"—may startle you. It's intended to. Typically we would think about meditating on the passion as bringing you *higher*—into the loftiest and most profound space of heart communion with Christ. But our author's trenchant insight here begins to make sense once you realize that what's descending is *your level of consciousness,* the power of your recollected attention. Let's see what happens next.

> And there he will let you see the wonderful kindness of God, and if you hear him out, he likes nothing better. For soon after that, he will let you see your old wretched way of living, and perhaps in seeing and reflecting on it, he will bring to your mind some place where you've lived in before this time. So at last, you are scattered, you know not where. The cause of this scattering is that you first listened to him willfully, answered him, received him, and gave him free rein [literally, 'allowed him']. (7-2)

Carmen Acevedo Butcher's translation is brilliant in its description of this descent. Here is her version of these two paragraphs:

> It [the thought] likes nothing better than to grab your attention, and once it knows you're listening, the thought will start rambling. It will chatter on about Christ's

Passion, drawing you in more and more, and then it will show you God's miraculous, sacrificial kindness. The thought loves it when you listen to it. Next, it will let you see how you used to live, when you were miserable and sinful, and as you begin thinking on those days, it will help you visualize where you lived at that time, and before you know it, *your mind is scattered all over the place.*[1] [italics added]

Note how in this descent our attention moves from conscious and voluntary to passive and associative, swirling around like a weathercock at every passing breeze, every new mental suggestion. When our attention becomes passive, the scattering and dissipating of our reservoir of spiritual attentiveness (known in Christian tradition as "recollection") is virtually guaranteed. It's like pulling the plug in a bathtub; the precious water of our gathered attention quickly drains away.

The author simply suggests that we not take the bait in the first place. No matter how pious or innocent a thought may be, as soon as the attention runs out to meet it, we are on a slippery slope toward inner scattering, the disintegration of our gathered presence.

Centering Prayer as Contemplative Laboratory

Admittedly, our author is setting the bar high here—so high that it's tempting to simply give up. Centering Prayer can help bridge the gap by bracketing this total-immersion training in objectless awareness within the periods of Centering Prayer itself, rather than attempting to take it on as a 24/7 practice. If you can simply remain faithful to the discipline of dismissing all thoughts during your daily twenty- to thirty-minute periods of meditation, the neural rewiring will gradually fill in that will allow you to stabilize heart cognition as your default mode of perception. But this takes time and will happen of its own accord, gently and integrally. Till then, you can best assist the work not by misguided efforts to have no thoughts during your normal working day, but simply through a willingness to promptly acknowledge and release conditioned patterns, hidden agendas, and polarized thinking whenever you realize you've fallen into them.

Our author is no polemicist. He understands very well the gradual and progressive nature of our capacity to stabilize a different kind of consciousness, and he repeatedly affirms the necessity of cataphatic prayer and moral self-examination as a foundation for this new kind of consciousness:

> And yet, nevertheless, the thing that he [the thought] said was both good and holy: yes, and so holy that any man or woman who thinks to come to contemplation without first having made many such sweet meditations on their own wretchedness, the Passion, the kindness, and the great goodness and worthiness of God is sorely mistaken and shall fail in his purpose. And yet, nevertheless, it behooves a man or woman who has been used to these meditations for a long time to consistently leave them and put them down under the cloud of forgetting if ever he is to pierce the cloud of unknowing between himself and his God. (7-3)

But once we have entered the contemplative training ground, it's important to be very clear about our aim—at least within the laboratory of Centering Prayer—and not get caught in the push-pull between two different modes of percep-tion. This is the reason for the apparent intransigence of our author's instructions. Once we set our "naked intent" upon entering this new field of perceptivity, it is critically important not to get lulled back into old attentional patterns.

> Therefore, at whatever time that you commit yourself to this work and feel by grace that you are called by God, then lift up your heart to God with a meek stirring of love. And understand by this the God who made you and bought you and has graciously called you to this work: and accept no other thought of God. And yet not even this is necessary unless you want to, for a naked intent to God suffices in itself, without any other cause but himself. (7-4)

"A Litil Worde of o' Silable"

The more mental and emotional complexity the thought carries, the more surface area there is for our attention to grab onto. This is why our author recommends keeping our prayer word short and concentrated—the instruction that launched the practice of Centering Prayer:

> And if you would like to have this word gathered and folded into one word in order to have a better hold on it, take but a little word of one syllable; for one is better than two, for the shorter it is, the better it accords with the work of the spirit. Such a word is the word GOD or the word LOVE. Choose whichever you will, or another if you like, whichever one-syllable word you like best. And fasten this word to your heart, so that it never leaves it no matter what might befall. (7-5)

Centering Prayer practitioners will of course be quick to pick up that the original instructions here have been modified slightly: in the contemporary method of Centering Prayer, words of two and three syllables and even short phrases ("Let go," "Be here," "Trust love") are all perfectly admissible. But the underlying principle remains unchanged: the shorter it is, "the better it accords with the work of the spirit."

Aficionados of the Johnston edition should note that here is another of those places where subtle but important misinterpretations have been introduced in the translation. Our *Cloud* author does *not* say, "Choose a word which is meaningful to you," as Johnston translates. He says, "Choose whichever one-syllable word you like." The two are not the same. And he does not say, "Fix the word in your mind"; he says, "Fix it in your *heart*"—a small but crucial difference as we try to trace our author's implicit awareness of the heart as the seat of nondual perception.

The question as to whether the sacred word should be personally meaningful is still one of those areas in Centering Prayer pedagogy where there are distinct differences between the various schools of interpretation. Father Basil Pennington placed great importance on the fact that the word is a "love word," as he called it, filled with both cognitive and emotional intent—in fact, encompassing the breadth and depth of one's affective relationship with God in a single, highly concentrated capsule. In this respect, his teaching falls clearly in line with the classic pedagogy of monastic love mysticism; his love is simply being expressed in a more concentrated form. In the Thomas Keating school of Centering Prayer, the word progressively becomes simply "a placeholder for your intention"; it carries that "naked intent direct to God" without any additional cognitive or emotional baggage. In fact, according to Keating, such additional baggage can subvert the intent of the prayer by *stimulating* thinking or self-reflection.

Which interpretation comes closer? Having been formed

myself in the Keating school, it is no surprise that I gravitate to this end of the interpretive spectrum. But over and above any factor of loyalty to my teacher, my rationale here is that I have noticed consistently over three decades now that the place where people are most likely to get stuck in Centering Prayer is around an oversolicitous relationship with their sacred word: it becomes too precious, too "all about me," too laden with spiritual expectation. Thus, it can tend to retard people at the level of the small self "doing" the prayer correctly rather than catapulting them directly into that underlying "naked intent," the true ground of both their prayer and their selfhood. People get bogged down when they try to make the word "too meaningful." So for the record, it's important to note that nowhere does our medieval author stipulate that the word needs to be meaningful. It merely needs to be palatable—and short.

Spiritual Warrior

This word shall be your shield and spear whether you ride in peace or in war. With this word you shall beat upon this cloud and this darkness above you. With this word you shall smite down all manner of thoughts under the cloud of forgetting insofar as, should any thought press upon you to ask you what you would have, you are to answer him with no more words than this one word. And if he offers you out of his great erudition to expound that word for you and to tell you all the conditions of that word, say that you prefer to have it whole, not broken and undone. And if you hold fast to this purpose, you can be certain that he will not tarry long. And why? Because you will not let him feed himself on such sweet meditations as described before. (7-6)

As you've probably gathered by now, I am more than a little ambivalent about this final paragraph of chapter 7. Certainly my job as a teacher of Centering Prayer would have been made considerably easier if he'd simply called it good with the instruction to "fasten this word in your heart." Aside from the overall negative impact of the militaristic imagery itself, it has led many practitioners—and for a time Keating himself[2]—to the conclusion that word is to be used to beat down or absorb all other thoughts rather than as a simple tether for one's intention, around which the thoughts may come and go. Our author is not fully consistent on this point himself, and it is in places like this that one finds oneself invoking the rather lame bailout clause that Centering Prayer is *based* on *The Cloud of Unknowing;* it is not a literal reproduction of it. Once again (as in *Cloud* 6), our author's real intent beneath the warrior imagery is to call forth the qualities of firmness and resolve rather than aggression and violence ("stalworthly" is the Middle English adverb used to describe this quality in *Cloud* 6—literally, "stalwartly"). And notice that while the word may indeed beat upon the cloud of unknowing in the depths of that "naked intent," its specific function is to "smite down all thoughts under the cloud of forgetting," or in other words, to sweep the decks clean. In that respect, then the meaning aligns with our present understanding of Centering Prayer. And our author's amazing touché of a rejoinder to this pesky thought—"tell him that you prefer your word whole, not broken or undone"—again demonstrates his intuitive grasp of the pulverizing and dissective properties of attention in its usual subject/object configuration. Not only his word but his field of consciousness he prefers to have whole.

For a final time it is necessary to correct a misimpression created by the Johnston edition. Nowhere does our *Cloud* author say, as the Johnston edition has it, that the thoughts will vanish "because you have refused to develop them with arguing."[3] Arguing is not the issue here. The issue is the seduction of cataphatic meditation, which pulls the mind out of its state of objectless recollection and into narrative and emotional pathos. This is the point our author will develop with painstaking thoroughness in our following chapter.

CHAPTER 12

The Art of
Contemplation (Cloud 8)

If you're a practitioner of Centering Prayer, even a beginning one, it will have been indelibly etched in your mind that contemplation is "resting in God." This is the beautiful, simple explanation condensed by Thomas Keating from a teaching by Pope Gregory the Great (540–604). This "resting" implies a movement beyond all thinking, emoting, sensing, and self-reflection to a simple presence, which Keating likes to evoke in terms of that beautiful line in Psalm 133: "Lord, I keep my soul at peace like a weaned child in mother's arms."

Like all beginning truths, however, this one is a bit of a simplification. It is certainly true that contemplation involves moving beyond the usual cataphatic practices of the mind and the sense of selfhood that rests on them. But the implication that contemplation is therefore content-free is a misperception that has led many modern Centering Prayer practitioners to an underestimation at best—and a distortion at worst—of the profound, indeed numinous awe accorded this state in the mysticism of both the Christian East and Christian West. In the traditional mystical assessment, contemplation is never simply a synonym for the *via negativa,* the pathway of pure emptiness; it is traditionally associated with a kind of seeing or "beholding" that is of a different order of intensity altogether. In the Hesychasm of the Christian East, this is typically associated with a direct *seeing* of God, a knowing from the *nous,* or "higher intellect," that involves the reunification of mind and heart at a level far beyond either mental or emotional cognition. In the West, the affective aspects of this inner unification are emphasized. Contemplation is a gift that emerges through "union with God," typically interpreted as "mystical marriage"; it is a profoundly beatific realization of Oneness attained. In both East and West, the stable attainment of this state is seen as an extraordinary gift, the maturation of a long journey of inner purification and preparation. That is why you will often see traditionally trained Christian contemplatives gritting their teeth when folks who are managing to sit on their prayer mats for twenty minutes twice a day confidently call themselves "contemplatives." Contemplation is not the automatic "perk" of a meditation method you do; it is the fruit of long journey into a completely different order and intensity of perception.

Once again, I would suggest that this traditional conundrum (just what *is* contemplation, anyway?), long exacerbated by the effusive language in which the state is usually presented, can be clarified by aligning contemplation with the state of nondual perception. Contemplation is by no means contentless; it's "merely" that this content is perceived and organized by the brain in a radically different way that requires the suspension or overriding of the normal cataphatic faculties. Out of this state of cataphatic emptiness emerges either a divine speaking/seeing (vision, revelation, mystical utterance) or else a profound apophatic silence, which itself speaks volumes.

As the Western thread insists, contemplation does indeed imply spiritual union. But this is not an *affective* union; rather, it is a perceptual erasing of the operating system that created

the differentiation in the first place. "You" drop out and
"God" drops out; there is only Oneness. And this Oneness
is experienced as intimate and personal because it is indeed
being perceived through the heart (purified and activated as
an "organ of spiritual perception"), and intimacy is the heart's
native language.

In other words, "contemplation" in the West is the functional equivalent of stabilized nondual consciousness in the
East. It is not a state of undifferentiated emptiness, but rather
a state of profound, luminous awareness in which the individual components are suffused and drawn together by a single
radiant Oneness, like light pouring through a stained-glass
window.

Amazingly enough, our fourteenth-century author seems to
have been on to this notion, and in the chapter we are about
to consider (*Cloud 8*) he lays out his argument in a way that,
once you see what he's up to, literally takes your breath away.
In his stunningly original portrayal of "the four degrees of
contemplative life" you can clearly detect a foreshadowing of
contemporary road maps of the levels of consciousness. For
in fact, these four "degrees" comprise, essentially, a ladder of
ascending self-reflective consciousness whose levels are subtly
delineated and strategically intertwined.

Let's have a closer look.

"A Good Thing or an Evil?"

> But now you ask me: "What is he, this that thus presses
> upon me in this work? And is it is a good thing or an
> evil?" "And if it be an evil thing, then I am amazed,"
> you say, "as to why he will increase a man's devotion so
> much. For sometimes I think it is a considerable com-
> fort to listen to his tales. For he will sometimes make
> me weep full heartily for pity of the Passion of Christ,

sometimes for my own wretchedness and many other reasons, that seem to me to be very holy and have done me much good. And therefore it seems to me that he can in no way be evil. And if he is good, and with his sweet tales does me such good, then I wonder why you bid me to put him down and away so far under the cloud of forgetting." (8-1)

Our author takes up the discussion exactly where he left off in chapter 7: if this thought pressing upon me seems to be increasing my devotion and spiritual awareness, then why let "him" go? What harm is done by receiving it and working with it?

Acknowledging that this is a good question, he proceeds to clarify that the chief operative in the emergence of these thoughts is "a sharp and clear perception by your natural capacities expressed in your reason within your soul" (literally, "a sharp and clear beholding of your natural mind expressed in your reason within your soul"). In other words (using the terminology I have been developing here) it is the cataphatic faculties making sense of the world by their inbuilt programming of "perception through differentiation." In and of itself, this is not a bad thing, but due to the inherent limitations of its operating system, it can cut in two directions. In the words of the old Sufi maxim, "a knife is neither good nor bad, but woe to him who grips it by the blade." It is good, our author agrees, when it is illumined by grace and allows one to grow in humility, devotion, and wonder, but evil when swollen by pride and earthly vanity. In this respect he both echoes and anticipates a long line of Christian mystical masters who will issue an identical warning.[1]

But our author does not let matters lie here. In an attempt to flesh out more fully this paradox of why the use of this natural capacity of the mind can be good in some circumstances and bad in others, he proceeds to present what can be recognized as the earliest map of the levels of consciousness known in the West:

> And where you ask me why you shall put it [the thought] down beneath the cloud of forgetting since it is good in its nature when it is well used and does you so much good and increases your devotion so much, to this I answer and say to you: there are two kinds of lives in the holy church. One is the active life, and the other is the contemplative life. The active is the lower and the contemplative is the higher. The active life has two degrees: a higher and a lower. And the contemplative life also has two degrees: a lower and a higher. And these two lives are coupled together in such a way that although they are different in some ways, yet neither of them may be had without some part of the other because the higher part of the active life is at the same time the lower part of the contemplative life. Because of this, a man may not be fully active unless he is partly contemplative. Nor may he be fully contemplative (as it may be had here) unless he is in part active. The condition of the active life is such that it is both begun and ended in this life. But not so the contemplative life, for it is begun in this life and shall last without end, for the part that Mary chose[2] shall never be taken away. Active life is troubled and worried about many things, but contemplative life sits in peace with one thing. (8-3)

For a brief moment our author allows us to think that he is simply going to resort to the clichéd dichotomy between the active and contemplative life. But immediately he pulls the rug out from under us by subdividing each category into two parts, higher and lower. This yields up a fourfold schematic: lower-active, higher-active, lower-contemplative, higher-contemplative. And then, as if to confound schematization altogether, he collapses the two middle rungs into a single overlapping ground, so that in place of four separate strata we have a chain-link fence! On this schematic he will unfold his remarkable teaching.

This chapter is of course good news for those working to move beyond the traditional polarization between active and contemplative as alternative lifestyles. About as explicitly as possible, our author makes clear that each one is embedded in the other and that no level can be fully attained or expressed without the active enfolding of the others. It is a wonderful intuitive glimpse at what six centuries later Ken Wilber will define as "transcend and include." Even at the highest level, our author avers, the active is not left behind, for a person "cannot be fully contemplative unless he is in part active."

Because the active life is so closely tied to the conditions of our earthly existence—including, as we shall see, that finite sense of selfhood and the cataphatic faculties that drive it—it comes to the end of its term with one's physical death. The contemplative life, which is not tied to the space/time dimensionality generated by this cataphatic operating system, is thus not subject to these term limits. But note, almost as an aside, how our author slips in the crucial information that the contemplative life, "chain-linked," as it were, to our natural and active one, must be begun in this life. In this he joins the tiniest handful of Western teachers who insist that contemplation is not a "perk" attained at one's death; the very purpose of our human life is to begin to lay down those foundational building blocks of unboundaried perception. Earthly life is the womb of nondual consciousness.

The Birth of Self-Reflection

Our author then proceeds to describe each of these four degrees:

> The lower part of the active life consists of good and honest bodily works of charity and mercy. The higher part of the active life and the lower part of the contemplative life lie in good spiritual meditations and diligent looking into [literally, "beholding"] a man's own wretchedness with sorrow and contrition, [looking] into the Passion of Christ and his servants with pity and compassion, and into the wonderful gifts, kindnesses, and works of God in all of his creatures both bodily and spiritual with gratitude and praise. But the higher part of contemplation (as it may be had here), hangs all holy in this darkness and in this cloud of unknowing, with a loving stirring and a blind beholding into the naked being of God himself only. (8-4)

He then adds as a further clarification:

> In the lower part of the active life a man is without himself and beneath himself. In the higher part of the active life and lower part of the contemplative life a man is within himself and even with himself. But in the higher part of the contemplative life a man is above himself and under his God. Above himself he is, because he intends to win by grace what he cannot come to by nature: that is to say, to be knit to God in spirit and in oneness [literally, "onehood"] of love and accordance of will. (8-5)

If we examine these three degrees, we realize that we are face-to-face with a threefold map of consciousness whose center point is in the emergence of the self-reflective capacity. In lower-active, a person is living on autopilot, so to speak, going through the external motions required by faith and by life, but without an introspective dimension. He is thus "beneath himself," not yet living at that self-reflective level in which the interior life begins to open up.

At higher-active/lower-contemplative the self-reflective capacity emerges, and in this awakening, "a man is within himself and even with himself." He awakens into a conscious relationship with his own interiority, and the seeds of the higher stage begin to appear. The "I think, therefore I am" gene awakens in him, along with a deepening capacity to read the road maps of the spiritual life from within.

This is the stage for which the vast bulk of Christian cataphatic practice is beautifully aimed. It is here that the traditional practices of meditation, *lectio divina,* "examen of conscience," praying the rosary, Ignatian discernment, walking the stations of the cross, and so much else are aimed: toward the development and stabilization of that awakened interiority.

But there is yet a higher level of consciousness attainable. And while our author describes it using his familiar stock of metaphors ("cloud of unknowing," "blind stirring of love," "a blind beholding of the naked being of God himself"), the schematic itself provides some valuable new context clues. We know, explicitly, that our author sees this as a higher level of consciousness, and it is higher precisely insofar as (1) the person is "above himself"—that is, above the level of self-reflective consciousness—and (2) that this level is characterized by "onehood"—a full alignment of spirit and will. Note that our author specifies an "accordance" of wills rather than a *union* of wills. The nuance is tiny but significant in that we see he is not imagining two different entities coming together in an affective union, but rather a kind of "blind beholding" (a classic understanding of contemplative perception) that overrides and darkens the cataphatic faculties but somehow still sees. The clues are strong that this contemplative state is here envisioned not simply as the unitive state classically understood but *as a different kind of perceptivity that suspends and transcends the self-reflective faculty.*

There are many remarkable aspects to this schematic, but certainly one of the most striking is how closely it matches the scenario we see actually being played out around us in our culture today. Recovery, wellness, and mindfulness are the secular buzzwords of our times, and it is clear that the heart of the action is unfolding right there at the higher-active level, with that sudden awakening to one's own interiority. Whether through psychotherapy, men's work, AA, yoga, mindfulness for stress reduction, enneagram work, dream work, soul work, or a host of other modalities, contemporary men and women are awakening to the realization that life is indeed an inner journey as well as an outer one. While these movements are overwhelmingly secular in expression (leading one to wonder whether the church's biggest institutional failure has been its incapacity to build the bridge between lower-active and higher-active, that is, from external observances to conscious interiority), our author's map assures us that this "failure" is understandable because the impetus properly originates in the active, or secular, quadrant of this overlapping circle. Once established there, it will morph naturally toward lower-contemplative as those wellness issues become less tied to preserving the small self and more tied to opening a far wider gamut of spiritual inquiry. The author's intuitive awareness of a "conveyor belt" aspect to this progress,[3] where each stage anticipates and in a way calls forth the next, is again a profoundly contemporary intuition. It suggests further that the key strategy for nurturing this wondrous and sensitive ground is to keep the circle intact: not dividing the territory into "secular" and "spiritual" sectors, but celebrating the entire gamut as a unified sphere of inner awakening.

Navigating the Rungs

With this master metaphor in place, our author is now brilliantly set up to deal with the question as to why good practices may no longer be helpful: because they belong to different rungs on the ladder and what supports one stage may become counterproductive at the next. Again, a truth readily demonstrated in life.

> And just as it is impossible to man's understanding to come to the higher part of the active life if he does not cease for a time the lower part, so it is that a man shall not come to the higher part of the contemplative life unless he ceases for a time the lower part. (8-6)

Thus, as good and worthy as they may be in their own right, the meditations and cataphatic/self-reflective practices must be let go for a time in order to pave the way for this higher-contemplative opening. For these practices correspond to the lower-contemplative, and if contact with them is prolonged during this transition to a whole different mode of perception, they will drag one back to the operating system and sense of selfhood appropriate to that lower form of consciousness. Seen from the schematic of advancing stages of consciousness, our author's instructions here make perfect sense.

As I stated at the beginning of this chapter, the Christian mystical tradition attests unanimously that contemplation is something special, a rare and luminous attainment in the spiritual life, which is usually seen as bearing fruit only after a long journey of spiritual preparation. What makes *The Cloud of Unknowing* such a groundbreaking work in the phenomenology of consciousness is our author's implicit awareness that this attainment so typically portrayed as a "gift" of increasing affective union with God is in fact *the leading edge of a higher kind of consciousness beyond self-reflection,* and that stabilization of this state has to do with the suspension of the practices that maintain the natural or cataphatic operating system of the mind. We stare here at the West's first taxonomy of consciousness, which implicitly links contemplation with what six centuries later will be termed "third tier" or non-dual consciousness.[4] It is far more concrete, practical, and in its own way *quantitative* than anything that will follow for several centuries.

For this reason, our author concludes,

> I bid thee put down such a sharp and subtle thought and cover him with a thick cloud of forgetting, no matter how holy he may be or how much he may promise to help you reach your purpose. And this is because love may reach God in this life but not knowledge. (8-7)

That "love" word again . . . But at this point we are beginning to bear down much more closely on our author's meaning. Clearly the "knowledge" he is talking about here is the conceptual knowledge based on the exercise of the cataphatic faculties. This may be good in and of its own right, but it belongs to the modality of that higher-active/lower-contemplative ground, which can no more access that realm of divine intercommunion than an old Underwood typewriter can access the Internet. A stronger operating system is needed: something that perceives and apprehends in a different way. And for this different kind of perceptivity, the word "love" still comes closest to hitting the mark. In the next section he will fill in a few more crucial pieces of the puzzle as to what this love is all about.

CHAPTER 13

The Mystery of Love
(Cloud 13–23)

Embedded in this first third of *The Cloud of Unknowing* is a remarkable set of chapters which I call "The Magdalenic Sequence." Cumulatively they paint a portrait of Mary Magdalene so unparalleled in its spiritual acuity and so distinctly modern in its presentiments that it's amazing how contemporary Magdalene aficionados have consistently overlooked them. Slowly but inexorably our author builds his case for Mary Magdalene as the *type*—the iconic embodiment—of the kind of transfigured love he has been trying to evoke for us throughout these opening chapters. If you get *her,* you'll get what he's talking about, and vice versa. Moreover, his intuition of the mutuality of her relationship with Jesus and the psychological insight he brings to describing this deeply interpenetrating spiritual love are also distinctly modern in flavor and should leave Madgalene devotees cheering. From the lineaments of the medieval Mary Magdalene (penitent whore, sinful woman) he is able to tease out the authentic perfume of conscious love.

And yes, alas, it *is* indeed the medieval Magdalene we are looking at here: that traditional conflated portrait casting her as whore, penitent sinner, recovering demoniac, and one and the same with Mary of Bethany, who sat at Jesus's feet in rapt devotion during preparations for the dinner party in his honor (Luke 10:38) and thus earned for herself (and her contemplative vocation) the designation "the one who has chosen the better part." Present-day scholarship, of course, largely rejects this composite portrait. The allegation of whoredom has now been formally repudiated as the sixth-century innovation of Pope Gregory I.[1] Debate still rages as to whether Mary Magdalene and Mary of Bethany are the same person (I am among those who still strongly believe that this traditional conflation is valid), and the jury is still out as to whether the alleged exorcism of her seven demons ever took place and, if so, what it signifies (healing of a mental illness or a profound spiritual initiation). But in any case, none of this is on our medieval author's radar screen. He plunges right into the traditional Magdalenic territory and works the turf like the profound spiritual maestro that he is. If you can push through any initial reactions to the stereotypic medieval Magdalene, what follows, I assure you, is a far cry from stereotypic.

Can Contemplation Make You Sinless? (Cloud 12)

The opening salvo for this actually begins in chapter 12 (and it is indeed a minor bombshell!) when our author returns to a claim he has already insinuated in chapter 3 and now hits it explicitly and forcefully. Among all the spiritual arts contemplation holds a unique place because "it is the work that destroys the ground and root of sin."

Can it possibly be true? This is, of course, a bold claim for the contemplative life and brings with it a massive risk of spiritual hubris and self-deception. But if you read the fine print carefully, you'll see that the claim being made here is actually more modest—and considerably more demanding:

If you wish to stand and not fall, therefore, never cease in your intent, but beat evermore on this cloud of unknowing that is between you and your God with a sharp dart of longing love. And be loath to think on anything that is under God, and do not leave no matter what. For this only, by itself, is that work that destroys the ground and the root of sin. (12-1)

Our author is being very specific here (and having worked our way through *Cloud* 3, 5, 6, 7, and 8, we are now in a position to better appreciate that specificity). He is not making a blanket claim about the contemplative "lifestyle." Rather, he is discussing a specific practice, namely, "Do not think of anything that is under God"—that is, do not to let your thought run out to objects, bifurcating your attentional field. It is *this practice* that destroys the ground and root of sin, for it is precisely in the dissipative, outward tending of the imagination that sin begins. Simply proclaiming oneself a contemplative does not do the trick for this author; the litmus test is whether one can restrain the outward-tending proclivities of the attention and hold the field of objectless awareness, into which sin cannot enter because there is nothing for it to grab onto.

In fact, he proceeds to insist that by themselves the external practices—fasting, vigils, asceticism, and even bodily mutilation—do not eradicate the ground of sin because they fail to completely expose that small-self "I" who always has some stake in the matter, some vested self-interest. It is from this subtle self-referentiality, inherent in the self-reflective consciousness itself, that deception and dishonesty enter: "For no matter how many virtues a man may have without it they are always mingled with some dishonest intention." That is Progoff's translation of *Cloud* 12-2.[2] The Middle English in this case makes the point even more forcefully, as you will see (last sentence, below):

No matter how much you fast, no matter how much you stay awake, no matter how early you arise, no matter how hard your bed or scratchy your clothes—yes, even if it were permitted (which it is not) for you to put out your eyes, cut your tongue out of your mouth, stop up your ears and your nose, shear away your members and inflict every pain on your body that you might conceive: all this would help you nought. The stirring and rising of sin will yet be in you.

And what's more, no matter how much you may weep for sorrow over your sins or the Passion of Christ, or no matter how much you keep in mind the joys of heaven, what will it do for you? To be sure, it will bring you much good, much help, much, much profit, and much grace, but in comparison with this blind stirring of love, it brings but little help without this other. This [blind stirring of love] by itself is the best part of Mary, without all the others. Those who are without it gain little or nothing. It not only destroys the ground and root of sin, as it may be here, but it gains virtues in this regard. For if it is truly understood, all virtues should be sweetly and perfectly comprehended and felt within it, without any mingled [literally, "meddling"] of your own intent. For no matter how many virtues a man may have without it, they have all been mingled with some crooked intent which makes them imperfect. (12-3)

From the context clues here, we now are able to sense more precisely what our author has been intending by this word "blind" (as in "blind stirring of love"). It clearly means *free from the interference of the self-reflective "I," which is always subtly co-opting and colonizing things for its own purposes.* A "blind" stirring of love takes place in that higher-contemplative bandwidth, where a person is "above himself and under his God"—or in other words, conscious within the sphere of objectless awareness rather than through the self-reflective mechanism that drives the dualistic sense of selfhood. Notice in the paragraph above that he is already likening this blind stirring of love to "the best part of Mary" (Magdalene, that is), laying the first strand in his weaving. From here he will shortly introduce his main topic for the next three chapters—and his entrée into his discussion of Mary Magdalene—through the question of virtue, particularly the virtue of meekness.

Perfect and Imperfect Meekness *(Cloud 13–15)*

Our Magdalenic sequence properly gets under way in chapter 13 with a discussion of the difference between "perfect" and "imperfect" meekness. While this may at first seem like an oblique lead-in, its relevance to the question at hand—how God may be "reached and held close by love"—will soon become fully apparent.

Meekness—or *humility,* if you prefer—is, according to our author, primarily about *self-knowledge.* "Meekness in itself is nothing else but a true knowing and feeling of a man's self as he is," he explains (13-2). It is not about external behaviors—definitely not about obsequious or self-deprecating mannerisms. It is quintessentially an *inner orientation,* the inevitable fruit of having come into relationship with the true north of one's selfhood. Beyond ego neediness and ego inflation is simply the naked ground of being—"the root of the root of yourself," in the words of the poet Rumi—and when one breaks into this primordial ground, all pretension simply drops away.

There are two ways of cultivating this meekness, according to our author. Both are good and necessary, but they belong to completely different orders of reality.

The first, which he calls "imperfect meekness," is developed by the earnest reflection on one's own sins and shortcomings. What in classic spiritual practice has been known as "scrupulosity" or "examen of conscience" may today be more familiar packaged as "making a moral inventory"—but in any case, the bottom line is the same. To the degree that you can honestly search out and "own" your own selfish and hurtful behaviors, you are able to cut others some slack. Entitlement and self-importance soften; in their place comes a deepening sense of solidarity with others in our common human fragility.

And this is important work, our author reminds us, from which we never "graduate." In fact, without it, the permanent stabilization of a state of perfect meekness is impossible:

> For though I call it imperfect meekness, yet I would rather have a true knowing and feeling of myself a wretch as I am, and I believe that it would acquire for me the perfect cause and virtue of meekness sooner by itself than if all the saints and angels in heaven, and all the men and women of the holy church living on earth, religious or seculars in all degrees, were to set out all at once together and do nothing else but pray to God for me to acquire perfect meekness. Yes, for without this [imperfect meekness] it is impossible for a sinner to acquire, or keep once it is acquired, the perfect virtue of meekness. (14-1)

The second kind of meekness, which he calls "perfect," emerges from a different source altogether. It comes from suddenly grasping the true scale of things, from a *felt sense* of the immensity of the cosmos and the vastness of divine love, against which all our human dramas and strivings become merely dust specks—"in the beholding of which all nature quakes, all scholars are fools, and all saints and angels are blind," as he picturesquely puts it (*Cloud* 13-2). It is the heart aching with the power of the infinite, recognizing that it is I myself—that slender veil of my created selfhood—that hides the paradise I seek.

A good example of perfect meekness (which our author, however, does not mention) can be seen in the final chapters of the book of Job. Throughout the entire preceding ordeal, Job has staunchly maintained his innocence and God has staunchly maintained his silence. Finally God speaks, and his response is a stunning vindication of Job's integrity. But it is not a judicial kind of vindication, a "well done, thou good and faithful servant." Rather, God figuratively sweeps Job up on eagles' wings and gives him a personal tour of the vastness of the cosmos and the bottomless depths of divine creativity. Job is introduced to the true scale of things; his response—"I had heard of you by the hearing of the ear, but now my eye sees you; therefore I despise myself and repent in dust and ashes"—is a paradigmatic expression of perfect meekness.

Note that perfect meekness implies a *felt sense:* in modern terminology, a shift to heart cognition. Imperfect meekness is the domain of the mind: concerned with measuring, assessing, inventorying. Perfect meekness is intrinsically holographic; through sympathetic resonance, you simultaneously grasp both the whole and the part. This is supremely the domain of heart cognition.

Our author does not use these terms, of course. But our suspicion that what he means by "love" has something to do with the shift from mental, object-focused attention to the objectless, holographic resonance characteristic of heart perception is further strengthened when he sets forth his bold claim in chapter 14 (paragraph 4) that "a secret love pressed in purity of spirit upon this dark cloud of unknowing between you and your God truly and perfectly contains within it the perfect quality of meekness without any special or clear beholding of anything under God." Once you see that "love" seems to be his code word for heart cognition, the rest of the picture begins to fill in.

Not Easy, but Possible: Cloud *15*

Having introduced these two categories of meekness and emphasized their inextricable interrelatedness, our author then moves on in chapter 15 to establishing the correct relationship between them—and in the process, foreshadows the basic thrust of his argument:

> Trust steadfastly that there is such a perfect meekness as I spoke of, and that it may come to you, through grace, in this life. And I say this to confound the error of those who say that there is no more perfect cause of meekness than that which arises out of mindfulness of our own wretchedness and the sins we have committed in the past. (15-1)

It is precisely this claim that our author will attempt to refute, calling on Mary Magdalene as his "exhibit A."

Please note as you work your way through *Cloud* 15 that the "Our Lady Saint Mary" referred to in this chapter is Mary, the mother of Jesus, not yet Mary Magdalene.

"Surely Because She Loved Much": Cloud *16*

This chapter brings us both literally and figuratively to the heart of our discussion. The presentation in these five pungent paragraphs is so luminously insightful that it might well be considered the epicenter not only of the Magdalenic sequence, but in a way, of the entire book. If you stay with this chapter carefully, *lectio divina* style, you will begin to sense what our author is trying to convey by his foundational instruction to "lift up your heart in a meek stirring of love."

> When our Lord said to Mary [Magdalene] as the representative of all sinners who have been called to the contemplative life, "Your sins be forgiven thee," it was not only for her great sorrow, nor for her mindfulness of her sins, nor even for the meekness she had in beholding her own wretchedness. But why then? Surely because she loved much. Lo! Here may men see what a secret pressing of love may purchase from our Lord, before all other works that man may conceive. (16-1)

"Surely because she loved much." With this simple delineation, our author drops Mary Magdalene right into the heart of his perfect/imperfect meekness paradigm, and the ground he has been slowly tilling suddenly bears fruit. While she certainly has plenty on her plate in the "imperfect meekness" department, it is this other—this intimation of the true scale of things—that carries her through.

Unfortunately, in the Progoff edition the crucial third paragraph contains a mistranslation; the second sentence should read "Even though she may have felt a deep or strong sorrow for her sins." There is a stray double negative in the Progoff version—"even though she may *not* have felt a deep or strong sorrow for her sins" which completely obscures the meaning. Here's my raw translation of the Middle English:

> But how? Surely as Mary did. Even though she might not unfeel the deep, heartfelt sorrow for her sins—for all her lifetime she had them with her wherever she went, as it were, in a burden bound together and carried secretly in the hole of her heart in a manner never to be forgotten—nevertheless, it may be said and affirmed

by scripture that she had a more heartfelt sorrow, a more doleful desire, and a deeper despair, and that she languished more—almost to the point of death—for lack of love than for any remembrance of her sins. Do not wonder at this, for it is the condition of a true lover that the more he loves, the more he longs to love. (16-3)

As you can see, once this confusion is cleared up, the paragraph opens into an extraordinary reflection on the two orders of sorrow—"imperfect" sorrow caused by remorse over one's sins as opposed to "perfect" sorrow caused by bearing the unmediated pain of yearning. In a remarkably astute observation on the infinite capaciousness of love, he concludes, "Do not wonder at this, for it is the condition of a true lover that the more he loves, the more he longs to love." True love might be defined, in fact, as the capacity to bear infinite yearning.

The next paragraph is a Middle English classic. Virtually any modern translation (and Carmen Butcher's is by far the best here) winds up to some degree unintentionally gentrifying the unmitigated, swashbuckling earthiness of the original— and with it, the life-saving dollop of humor. Here's my raw text:

For sure, she knew well and felt it keenly in herself in a sad truthfulness that she was the most foul of all wretches and that her sins had made a division between herself and her God that she loved so much, and that they were in great part the cause of her languishing sickness for lack of love. But what thereof? Did she therefore come down from the height of desire into the depths of her sinful life and search in the foul, stinking swamp and dunghill of her sins, searching them out one by one with all their attending circumstances and sorrowing and weeping upon each one of them in itself?

No, surely she did not do so. And why not? Because God let her know by His grace within her soul that she should never bring it about this way. For had she done so, she might sooner have raised up in herself the ability to sin often than to have purchased by that work any clear forgiveness of her sins. (16-4)

Note the psychological acuity here, both in his understanding that the sins themselves were a substantial cause of her present suffering (as the old saying goes, "We are punished by our sins, not for our sins!") and in his realization that obsessing upon them would more likely energize than heal them—a fascinating medieval premonition of what we might nowadays recognize as victim psychology.

The final paragraph reveals the key to the mystery if you're willing to stay with it, pondering the extraordinary insights packed into each sentence:

And therefore, she hung up her love and her longing desire in this cloud of unknowing, and she learned to love a thing that she might never see clearly in this life, neither by the light of her understanding of her reason nor by a true feeling of sweet love in her affection. (16-5)

Note that she did not *renounce* her love and longing desire. She simply *let them go,* entrusting them into the gentle, enveloping wisdom of the cloud. This sentence essentially repeats a line we have already heard in chapter 3, but in the present context the meaning becomes much clearer. We are obviously not talking about reason versus emotions here; the love she feels is not "a true feeling of sweet love in her affection." It is beyond the cataphatic faculties altogether, inaugurating a whole new modality of perception.

> Very often, in fact, she had hardly any special remembrance of whether she had been a sinner or not. (16-5)

Self-reflection—that is, the mental capacity to stand outside oneself and view oneself as an object of one's attention—has dissolved, along with the mirage of selfhood thereby created. The subject/object poles of consciousness have reunited in a pure subjectivity.

> Yes, and I hope that she was very often so deeply immersed in the love of his Godhead that she hardly saw the details of the beauty of his precious and his blessed body in which he sat speaking and preaching before her with such great love. Neither did she see anything else, neither physical nor spiritual . . . (16-5)

Clearly, Mary Magdalene is in an "altered state of consciousness." But this is not simply mystical rapture, typically interpreted as an ecstatic emotional experience. In terms of the phenomenology of consciousness as our author has been steadily developing it, the chief feature of this mode of perception is that the subject/object dichotomy gives way to a diffuse awareness, in which one does not "see" anything in particular, but comes into full resonance with the infinite source of love. While this mode of perception (essentially the shift from head cognition to heart cognition) can overtake a person unexpectedly (as a "mystical experience"), it can also—preferably—grow into a steady mode of consciousness (Ken Wilber would call it a "stage" rather than a "state") that is not dependent on paranormal experiences but can be steadily cultivated as we learn to withdraw our attention from external objects and hold it poised and gathered within the waiting chalice of our heart. This repatterning of our attention is the essence of the "work" of contemplation as our author sees it, and its fruit is our initiation into the mystery of love.

Cloud *17–23*

Having attained the summit of the argument, the remaining chapters in the Magdalenic sequence settle down to "business as usual," cleaning up the remaining obligatory details. *Cloud* 7 reaffirms Mary Magdalene's traditional assignation as exemplar par excellence of the contemplative life, but now ties it specifically to her capacity to rest within the cloud of unknowing:

> For one thing I tell you: there has never yet been such a pure creature in this life, or ever will be one raised so high in contemplation and the love of the Godhead that there will not still remain a high and wonderful cloud of unknowing between him and his God. It was in this cloud that Mary was occupied with many a secret pressing of love. And why? Because it was the best and the holiest part of contemplation that may be had in this life. (17-2)

Chapters 18 through 21 work the familiar theological terrain contrasting Mary and Martha as respective models of the contemplative and active life. While our author's conclusions here are pretty much what you would expect, he manages to add in an interesting twist in chapter 21 when he ponders what it might mean when scripture tells us that Mary has chosen the *best* part? Reasoning that "best" is only relevant when there are *three* terms (good, better, and best), he uses this springboard to reprise his "threefold" model of the spiritual life first introduced in *Cloud* 8 (lower-active, higher-active/

lower-contemplative, higher-contemplative) and to reaffirm the primacy of the contemplative path.

Chapter 22 will come as a surprise and delight to contemporary Mary Magdalene aficionados attempting to tease out a love interest between Mary Magdalene and Jesus. Our author plunges right in, without hesitation: "Sweet was that love between our Lord and Mary [Magdalene]. Much love had she for him; much more had he for her" (22-1). Carmen Acevedo Butcher's brilliant translation of this passage is not only literally accurate, but in some ways even more evocative than the original:

The love our Lord and Mary Magdalene had for each other was sweet. She loved him so much, and he loved her even more. If you could have seen the looks that passed between them, you'd know. This isn't gossip; it's the Gospel.[3]

And the reasons for this conclusion? On Mary's part, because she loved Jesus so completely that even the angels couldn't comfort her when she sought him at the sepulcher on Easter morning: "For whoever seeks the King of Angels will not settle for angels." (!) And on Jesus's part, because "he would not permit any man or woman, even her own sister, to speak a word against her without answering for her himself" (22-3). Our author is clearly picking up on an energy in their relationship that is personal and deeply mutual, refusing to be contained by the teacher/disciple model within which it is traditionally circumscribed. Here again his spiritual insight is matched and deepened by his psychological acuity.

Cloud 23 brings the sequence to a close with a beautiful reflection on God's provident care for those who, like Mary Magdalene, seek the path of perfect meekness—for from this, all the rest will follow:

And therefore, you who set yourself to be contemplative as Mary was, choose rather to be humbled under
the wonderful height and worthiness of God, which is
perfect, than under your own wretchedness, which is
imperfect. That is to say, take care that your attention
is more on the worthiness of God than on your own
wretchedness. For to those that are perfectly humbled,
no thing shall be wanting, neither bodily nor spiritual.
They have God, in whom all abundance is, and who has
Him—yes, as the book tells us—needs nothing else in
this life. (23-4)

One hears here, of course, the direct foreshadowing of
those powerful lines penned by Teresa of Âvila two centuries
later, and now indelibly etched in hearts worldwide through
one of the most beloved of the Taizé chants:[4]

Nada te turbe, nada te'espante;
Quien a Dios tiene nada le falta.
Nada te turbe, nada te'espante,
Solo Dios basta.

Which translates to:

Let nothing trouble you, let nothing frighten you;
He who loves God lacks nothing.
Let nothing trouble you, let nothing frighten you;
God alone is enough.

By Way of a Conclusion

With this Magdalenic sequence, we come to the end of the
first third of *The Cloud of Unknowing*—and the completion
of our interpretive key. From the clues laid down in these early

chapters and brilliantly woven together in the living emblem of Mary Magdalene, you have all the pieces before you to continue the journey on your own, parsing out the additional instructions, refinements, and occasional readjustments according to the following basic glossary:

> *thought:* attention configured in the subject/object configuration.
>
> *creature:* any object of attention, no matter whether it is concrete or abstract, sentient or disembodied.
>
> *cloud of unknowing:* the author's chosen metaphor for diffuse, or objectless, awareness—that is, a mode of consciousness that can remain aware without a specific object of awareness. As such, it anticipates what we now call "nondual awareness."
>
> *cloud of forgetting:* the author's chosen metaphor for the discipline of letting go of objects of attention, returning the mind to its state of objectless awareness.
>
> *contemplative:* one who actively engages in the work of stabilizing the mind in a state of objectless awareness.
>
> *love:* a state of awareness grounded in feeling-resonance but unfettered by emotional affectivity, subject/object awareness, or a personal self-center. Love is the author's chosen metaphor for this distinctly different kind of perceptivity, holographic in modality and infinite in domain. Stabilizing this consciousness within oneself essentially confers immunity from the ravages of time and linearity: "For the soul is as truly there where its love is as it is in the body which lives by means of it and to which it gives life" (60-2). While our author demonstrates no systematic awareness that this alternative mode of consciousness is centered in the heart (in fact, he does not specifically address the heart anywhere in his text), he does obliquely make

the connection through his oft repeated instruction to "Lift up your *heart* in a meek stirring of love," in his recognition that the sacred word must be "fastened in your *heart*" (7-5), and in his recognition that this other mode of reality "can be better felt than seen" (68-4).

blind: free from the interference of the self-reflective "I," which is always subtly co-opting and colonizing things for its own purposes.

naked (as in "a naked intent direct to God"): not under the sway of the cataphatic faculties (memory, reason, emotion, will), but emerging from a deeper level of being within, which can neither be co-opted nor resisted.

meek stirring of love: the spiritual attentiveness emerging spontaneously from this deep inner wellspring.

The above glossary is intended to be suggestive, not exhaustive. But with this basic GPS at hand, I encourage you to wander deeper and deeper into this wondrous turf and explore a thinker whose sheer originality and brilliance become even more apparent when set free from the traditional categories of Christian love mysticism and seen as a rising star in the firmament of nondual awakening.

CHAPTER 14

Sorrow of Being
(Cloud 43–44)

In these past eighty pages we have technically covered only twenty-three chapters of *The Cloud of Unknowing* (well, *super-technically*, only eighteen, since I've skipped a few along the way), a little less than a third of the book. Yet these chapters lay down the foundation of the author's teaching, and my hope is that by having taken the time to explore them carefully, you'll find it pretty much smooth sailing through the rest of the *Cloud*.

Our author will circle back several more times to the key building blocks of his teaching. You'll find more on the use of the sacred word in contemplative prayer: why short is better, helpful suggestions for dealing with temptation during prayer, and some wise and remarkably well-grounded advice about the right stewardship of the body, particularly in the presence of strong ecstasy or strong yearning. He will warn us once again about the dangers of the undisciplined use of the imagination in this line of contemplative work and rail against those who believe they can reach God through their natural reasoning alone. And again and again he will sound the note of "perfect meekness" as the touchstone of the contemplative life.

You may find yourself thrown for a loop, however, when he slides into a section beginning in chapter 43 (and continuing in earnest in chapter 44), where he characterizes your core sense of personal selfhood as a "foul, stinking lump of sin" and encourages you to "destroy all knowing and feeling of your own being." To modern ears this inevitably sounds like a heavy dose of medieval self-hatred—aggravated, no doubt, by repression and spiritual bypassing! But if you can resist jumping too quickly to these conclusions, you'll see that our author is actually describing something a good deal subtler.

Here are some of the most notoriously troublesome passages:

> This shall you do with yourself: you shall loathe and be wary of all things that work in your mind and your will unless it be God. For surely anything else, no matter what it might be, is between you and your God. It is no wonder that you should loathe and hate to think on yourself, for you will always feel sin as a foul, stinking lump of you know not what between yourself and your God: the lump is none other than you yourself! You will perceive it as united [literally, "oned"] and congealed with the substance of your being, such that it will never leave you. (43-2)
>
> Therefore, break down all knowing and feeling of all manner of creatures, but most assiduously of yourself. For on the knowing and feeling of yourself hang the knowing and feeling of all other creatures, and the reward for accomplishing this is that all other creatures are easily forgotten. (43-3)

And:

All men have reason for sorrow, but most particularly does he have cause for sorrow who knows and feels that he is. Compared to this, all other sorrows are but games. (44-2)

And:

For as often as he seeks to have a true knowing and feeling of God in purity of spirit (as it may be had here), he realizes that he cannot, for he finds always that his knowing and feeling are occupied and filled with a foul, stinking lump of himself that must be hated and despised and forsaken if he is to be God's perfect disciple, realized on the mount of perfection. And whenever he sees this, he goes practically mad for sorrow. (44-3)

This "sorrow of being," as he calls it in chapter 44, is of an entirely different order of reality from personal guilt and shame. Just as we have earlier noted the difference between "imperfect" and "perfect" meekness, a parallel situation exists between what we might call "imperfect" and "perfect" sorrow. Guilt and self-hatred belong to the ballpark of "imperfect" sorrow; they grow out of an acknowledgment of one's own personal failures and culpability. But the "perfect" sorrow our author is evoking here is actually a *felt sense awareness* that you are *yourself* the veil that hides the paradise you seek. In an excruciating catch-22, you feel with your entire being how the very sword stroke that delivers you into individual consciousness and identity simultaneously separates you from the whole. As you explore this strange, unfamiliar territory with your heart cognition (it is inaccessible to your mind alone), you come to actually sense the space—*feel the weight*—that your created being takes up in the radiant and flowing field of divine love. You sense yourself—just as our author says—as a "lump," with volume and turbidity, and the result is almost always a sharp stab of sorrow. But it is not a personal sorrow, but rather a deeply luminous and transpersonal appreciation of the "cost" of divine love.

And it is, as our author reminds us, holy ground being traversed here: painful but purifying. For you are indeed standing at the outer boundary of consciousness itself, at least as far as it can be borne in finite flesh:

> This sorrow, when it is attained, cleanses the soul not only of sin but also of the pain that derives from sin. And because of this, it makes the soul able to receive that joy which removes from a man all knowing and feeling of his being. This sorrow, if it is truly conceived, is full of holy desire, or else a man in this life might not be able to endure or bear it. (44-2)

Nor is it to be confused with depression or, heaven forbid, suicidal tendencies:

> He thinks that he bears such a heavy burden of himself that he cares not a bit what becomes of him, so long as God is pleased. And yet in all this sorrow he does not desire to cease to exist [literally, to "un-be"], for this would be the devil's rage and spite for God. But he wishes very much to be and sincerely intends to thank God with all his heart for the gift and worthiness of his being, though he does desire unceasingly to be rid of the knowing and feeling of his being. (44-3)

Very few Christian writers, even at the mystical outposts, have explored this terrain, and when they do, they are almost always misunderstood. A classic example in our own times is Bernadette Roberts, whose description of her journey to "no-self" is almost always interpreted as a dropping of the ego-self, not a piercing of the veil of self-reflexive consciousness itself.

Thomas Merton is another contemporary mystic who in the final years of his life came to an acute appreciation of this state of "no-self." His brilliant but challenging reflection on *fana* ("self-annihilation" in Islamic mysticism), offered in the course of an ongoing correspondence with the Islamic scholar Abdul Aziz, covers virtually the same ground we have just traversed. I have quoted it already in connection with *Cloud* 6 (see page 154, but hear it again in this more all-embracing context:

> My prayer tends very much toward what you call *fana* [annihilation in God]. There is in my heart this great thirst to recognize totally the nothingness of all that is not God. My prayer is then a kind of praise rising up out of the center of Nothing and Silence. If I am still present "myself," this I recognize as an obstacle about which I can do nothing unless He Himself removes the obstacle. If He wills, He can make the Nothingness into a total clarity. If He does not will, then the Nothingness seems itself to be an object and remains an obstacle. Such is my ordinary way of prayer, or meditation. It is not "thinking about" anything, but a direct seeking of the Face of the Invisible, who cannot be found unless we become lost in Him who is invisible.[1]

If you can work your way patiently through this tough patch, the rest should fall together pretty straightforwardly— that is, if you keep always in the back of your mind that what we're really dealing with is a fourteenth-century fore-runner of what today would be called the phenomenology of consciousness—and specifically consciousness at that key transition point where it shifts from brain-centered to heart-centered cognition. In this respect, our medieval author is so far ahead of the curve that we're barely catching up. But armed with confirming evidence from neuroscience and a much more exact language to describe attention, objectless awareness, and heart cognition, we can marvel at how on-target our author's intimations actually are: a good advertisement, all told, for the kind of deeply intuitive knowing that is the fruit of committed contemplative practice.

The Elastic Universe (Cloud 4)

I said that I would return to *Cloud* 4 at the end of this book, so here we are.

In a way it's a pity that our medieval author inserted the material in this chapter so early in his book, sandwiched in between his more straightforward commentary in chapters 3 and 5. This chapter is a wild ride indeed! If you find it's leaving you totally bewildered, it's perfectly all right to skip to the last paragraph (which follows almost without a hiccup from the last paragraph of chapter 3), and from there right into chapter 5.

But if you're up for the detour, what lies before you is an extraordinary fourteenth-century foreshadowing of a concept that has come to full articulation only six centuries later. Essentially you are looking here at a medieval run-up on Einstein's theory of relativity, or the elasticity of time!

"Time was made for man, not man for time," our medieval author observes. But if this sounds like a familiar truism ("the Sabbath was made for man, not man for the Sabbath"), he certainly does not develop it along familiar lines. Instead, he lays out the remarkable proposition that time is a *function of the will*. It emerges in the form of distinct packets ("stirrings of the soul," as he calls them), one moment for each stirring. Carmen Acevedo Butcher's translation is brilliant here:

> And you should be held responsible for it [how you
> spent your time], because this briefest moment of time
> is exactly how long it takes your will, that strong arch-
> itect of your soul, to desire something and to act on
> that desire. In an hour you experience the same number
> of aspirations and cravings as there are atoms in that
> space and time, and if you were restored by grace to the
> original unity of your soul, you'd be the master of every
> impulse. You'd never feel out of control because every
> desire would be directed toward the most desirable and
> highest good, which is God.[1]

If you've ever noticed how time speeds up when you're flowing
with it and slows down almost to a snail's pace when you're in
resistance (like standing in a shopping line or enduring a boring
lecture), you've already tasted this principle of elasticity.

And the place where time speeds up the most, our author
claims—to the point that it essentially vanishes—is when you're
engaged in contemplation. Refuting the impression that this
work is time-consuming, he essentially claims that it only takes
a nanosecond! His reasoning is simple: when each stirring of
the will reunites with and is subsumed into the source of its
desiring, time drops outs. We are catapulted out of linearity
into an eternal now.

In this sense, contemplation—real contemplation, that is,
not woolgathering on the meditation mat—is essentially an "out
of time" experience. Time is swallowed up not by death but by
the complete reunion of wills.

What makes this chapter so challenging is that it's hard to
believe you're actually reading what you're reading! It's hard to
believe that an anonymous medieval mystic could have such an
uncannily contemporary notion of time. But if you sit with his
amazing insights with your analytical mind on "pause" and your
heart wide open, my hunch is that the picture will begin to fill in.

Going Forward

From start to finish my book has really been addressed in equal measure to two different groups: those of you who are practicing Centering Prayer and those of you who aren't. In these final pages, let me share a few parting thoughts with each group in turn.

For Practitioners

If you're a practitioner, you will probably already have noticed (no doubt with more than a little fear and trembling) that the Centering Prayer movement poises on the brink between two eras. The first generation of founders is mercifully still mostly with us, and the curriculum and organizational infrastructure developed by Contemplative Outreach have laid a firm foundation. But if the movement is really to survive and prosper—at least with the organicity it claims for itself[1]— it will need to be very much about the mission of nurturing a new generation of leaders who can grow and extend the teaching, not merely faithfully reproduce what has been received. That will take courage, flexibility, and a trust that those capacities for deep inner attunement already catalyzed by the practice will continue to bear fruit.

EMBODY, EMBODY, EMBODY!

In my opinion, the first priority facing a new generation of practitioners is the need for a deeper embodiment of the practice. There are still too many doing Centering Prayer in their heads, preoccupied with the correct application of "their" sacred word or struggling to achieve a thought-free inner state, which they equate with "consenting to the presence and action of God." Once the kenotic nature of the prayer is grasped and trusted—*really* grasped and trusted—all this falls away. As "letting go" becomes an embodied gesture rather than a spiritual attitude to be striven for during the meditation period, Centering Prayer immediately drops out of the head and into a resonant center in the middle chest region (heart to solar plexus). The mind quiets down since it is no longer burdened with worry. Performance anxiety also drops away, as the focus is no longer on creating inner stillness or any other spiritual desideratum, but simply on offering the release, in solidarity with Jesus's own kenotic heart. "Ten thousand opportunities to return to God!" The practice shifts from something you *perform* to something you *give*.

WHAT ABOUT THE BREATH?

This is a perennial issue in Centering Prayer teaching. Thomas Keating's challenging counsel to simply let the breath go, too (allowing it to become shallow or even intermittent), is so blatantly crosswise with virtually every other meditation path that even experienced practitioners tend to balk. And to be sure, since conscious breathing is in fact so foundational to consciousness, it is hard to concede that the Centering Prayer practice seems to make so little use of it. The perennial temptation is to try to combine Centering Prayer with some form of breath practice, typically by attaching a few deep breaths or even *several minutes* of conscious breathing to the beginning of the meditation period proper.

Having experimented with this myself over the years (remember that my early spiritual training was in the Gurdjieff Work, where conscious breathing is one of the mainstays), I have reached my own conclusion that it is perfectly acceptable for Centering Prayer practitioners to work with breath prayer, but not directly connected to the Centering Prayer period—*at least not to the beginning of it*. Once conscious breathing is introduced, the two attentional bandwidths fight with each other, breath bringing a more alert, "I am here" attention that retards the release into that complete state of inner letting go that is the signature modality of Centering Prayer. "I am here" presence is foundational in most meditation practices, but in Centering Prayer, it is the kenotic release that delivers the goods. You have to trust it, not hedge your bets.

In case you're curious, my own practice over the years has gradually evolved into a kind of hybrid that places the conscious breathing on the *back* end of the Centering Prayer period. For the twenty or so minutes that I am officially doing Centering Prayer, I offer it in complete kenotic release. Breath, attention, "I am here" presence: all is let go. Then (on most days) when the Centering Prayer period is over, I gradually shift into a version of the Jesus Prayer, saying on the inbreath, "Holy heart of God," and on the outbreath, "Lord Jesus Christ, have mercy on me." (My sacred word, "heart," makes this transition seamless.) All the while I am slowly bringing my attention to my breath and to the sensation of the invocation flowing through my heart. It makes for a very strong (and often moving) transition back into daily life.

I am by no means recommending this universally, and for some (those just embarking on Centering Prayer or who come to it with theological issues around their relationship to Jesus) I would definitely stay well clear of it. What makes Centering Prayer so clean is that it is simply twenty minutes of pure kenotic practice. Outside of those simple, well-defined boundaries, do as you please, and by all means work with breath and attention practices if you feel so moved. They certainly facilitate the capacity to incarnate that kenotic stance as you move out into daily life.

But in any haste to "supplement" Centering Payer, it might be well to simply cast an occasional sideways glance at Thomas Keating, whose breath has gone shallow during meditation for forty years and whose luminosity and fullness of being are there for all to see. It would be hard in his presence to maintain that Centering Prayer cannot get you there in and of itself.

NONDUAL PERSONHOOD

Another growing edge for an upcoming generation of Centering Prayer lies in the need for an updated and expanded understanding of personhood that matches the nondual trajectory of this prayer. Keating's "divine therapy," developed during the 1980s, is a powerful teaching aimed squarely at what our *Cloud of Unknowing* author would call the higher-active/lower-contemplative bandwidth. It acknowledges and nurtures the birth of self-reflective consciousness and leads practitioners on a liberating journey from false-self entrapment to high-egoic functioning. This teaching has been a literal lifesaver for thousands, dovetailing brilliantly with the contemporary recovery movement and paving the transition from psychotherapeutic models to authentic spiritual work. But the teaching is still pitched to that egoically generated, "narrative" self who all too often mistakes its hard-earned high-egoic functioning for the true self. I have watched Centering Prayer practitioners hung up on this issue—in some cases for decades!—and it's a pity, because the practice itself has already prepared them to move beyond it, into the bona fide higher-contemplative quadrant, where one is "above oneself and under one's God." Since Centering Prayer is headed toward nondual selfhood, anyway, it becomes paramount for a next generation of teachers to begin to set in place the conceptual framework to support this transition, including a greater attention on witnessing presence, objectless attention, and the capacity to live fully and wisely beyond personal storytelling and drama.

For Nonpractitioners

My apologies to you all if my message remains monotonously consistent. I hope this book has given you a better sense of Centering Prayer's distinctiveness and the principles from which it derives its integrity and efficacy. Judged by the usual expectations of a meditation practice, Centering Prayer does certainly look like an odd duck. It can be frustratingly fuzzy, sleepy, or spacey. People can and do daydream, sometimes for a long time, before that connection to their own deeper intentionality finally kicks in. But when judged within its own frame of reference, Centering Prayer begins to come into focus, and the method behind its apparent madness begins to make sense.

That focus, or course, is kenosis, the radical "self-emptying" or nonclinging that is for Saint Paul the very essence of "putting on the mind of Christ." At its bare-bones simplest, Centering Prayer is essentially "kenosis in meditation form," an entry-level but authentic participation in the mind of Christ through the concrete act of letting go of thoughts—that is, objects of attention. That is all Centering Prayer is about, but this "all" speaks volumes. Seen against this kenotic backdrop, its instructions become intelligible. Fears raised by Christian fundamentalists that Centering Prayer is simply narcissism writ large or by teachers of traditional Eastern methods that it leads to a permanent state of "sinking mind" prove to be equally misplaced. Yes, you will not find here that bandwidth of bright, clear attention so prized in spiritual traditions linking consciousness to luminosity. But when consciousness is linked to *intimacy*—the direct perception of a radiant "thou-ness" suffusing everything, drawing all things together in love—then we are looking at a different conceptual model altogether, one in which the primordial responses (even in meditation) are self-oblation and a bowing of the knee of the heart. Centering Prayer rises and falls on the strength of one's commitment to that model.

For Both Camps

This brings me to my final point. Surely it would be inaccurate to claim that this intimate, relational understanding of the highest states of conscious attainment is unique to Christianity. But it is certainly *foundational* to Christianity, the mainspring that makes everything else go. Too often, when Christianity's mystical tradition is examined under the lens of contemporary models of levels of consciousness, this personalizing, heart-centered perceptivity does not show well. It tends to be interpreted as a lower-level dualism, still firmly under the sway of personal desire and affectivity. What does not seem to register is that beneath all the effusive imagery of mystical marriage and beatific vision, what is really under discussion is not the state of attainment of the individual mystic, but *the nature of consciousness itself*. It is not cool but *warm*, claims the Western tradition—not impersonal or even transpersonal, but astonishingly *hyper*personal. "Pure intimacy," as Robert Sardello has it.

As most of you have by now, no doubt, deduced, my real concern in this book is not just with Centering Prayer, but with the interpretive window that Centering Prayer opens up on the entire Christian nondual tradition, arguably Christianity's best kept secret. My work with *The Cloud of Unknowing* has been a pilot project in this regard, and I hope that it paves the way for other such re-visioning efforts, which to my mind are long overdue. The territory is rich but still hidden beneath off-putting language and theological accretions. As we've seen with *The Cloud,* some decoding is in order.

For this work I am grateful to have at my disposal the new tools available to us from contemporary neuroscience, integral philosophy, and phenomenology. They give us a whole new way of framing the Christian mystical tradition, breaking it loose from its well-entrenched metaphysical perspectives and opening up important new lines of bearing for validation and interspiritual dialogue. To identify *The Cloud of Unknowing* as a pioneering study in the phenomenology of conscious-ness is a hypothesis that would have been impossible even twenty-five years ago; there would as yet have been no ground beneath my academic feet. And I hope you'll agree that its new assignation sheds far more light on our Christian nondual heritage than in its former role as merely another exemplar of Western affective mysticism.

But it is also important to keep in mind that these new road maps, having been derived largely from Eastern metaphysi-cal models, by and large do not do justice to Christianity's intuitively kenotic way of getting there. My first request in an effort to level the playing field would be for a new map of the levels of consciousness, one that portrays the nondual (Wilber's "third tier") not merely as an extension of the cognitive line, but as *an entirely new line,* branching off (most likely) from the cognitive line at the integral level[2] and making visually clear that the transposition of consciousness onto this line requires capacities opened up (or at least enhanced) through kenotic practice. These would include an overall spiritual intention of nonattachment combined with a physiological *descent* and *gathering* of energy in the region of the heart and solar plexus.

As these more closely honed research questions meet a steadily increasing technical sophistication in the field of neuroscience, I suspect that within the foreseeable future we will see an expanded road map of the journey to nonduality, together with a new way of evaluating and leveraging Christian mystical texts. Even the effusive love mysticism usually typecast in present maps of consciousness as belonging to a personalistic and therefore lower level of consciousness, I suspect actually contains the seeds, metaphorically, of that nonnegotiable Christian affirmation that luminosity is love; the two cannot be separated. And love requires the participation of the heart.

At any rate, with Centering Prayer readily available to deliver kenotic practice in a simple but very pure meditational format, the way is now open, just as with *The Cloud of Unknowing,* to go back to our classic Christian mystical texts and look at them through new eyes—and more importantly, a new heart.

NOTES

INTRODUCTION

1. Cynthia Bourgeault, *Centering Prayer and Inner Awakening* (Cambridge, MA: Cowley Publications, 2004. Now an imprint of Rowman & Littlefield Publishers Inc.)
2. Ira Progoff, ed., *The Cloud of Unknowing* (New York: Delta Books, 1957), p. 72.
3. See in particular, David Frenette, *The Path of Centering Prayer* (Boulder, CO: Sounds True, 2012), with its expanded and helpful treatment of the use of the sacred word.

OVERVIEW

1. Ira Progoff, ed., *The Cloud of Unknowing* (New York: Delta Books, 1957), p. 76.

CHAPTER 1. WHAT IS NONDUALITY?

1. I am assuming that most readers will be familiar with this map, which Wilber first launched in the popular market with his 1981 book *Up from Eden* (Wheaton, IL: Quest, 1981). He has continued to refine his work on the subject over the past thirty years now; the most recent

published version as of 2016 can be found in *Integral Spirituality* (Boston: Shambhala, 2006), overleaf to p. 68.

2. Thomas P. McDonnell, ed., *A Thomas Merton Reader* (New York: Doubleday/Image Books, 1989), p. 345.

3. Ken Wilber, *Integral Spirituality,* pp. 4–5. Basically, a state is a place you go to; a stage is a place you come from. A stage is a level of consciousness permanently attained and stabilized.

4. Raimon Panikkar, *Christophany* (Maryknoll, NY: Orbis Books, 2004), p. 44.

5. The threefold schematic was first developed by the sixth-century spiritual master Pseudo Dionysius and has exerted a foundational influence on both the Eastern and Western streams of Christian mystical understanding.

6. Beatrice Bruteau, "Prayer and Identity," in *Sewanee Theological Review* 50:3 (Pentecost 2007), p. 399. Later republished in the anthology *Spirituality, Contemplation, and Transformation* (New York: Lantern Books, 2008).

7. Wilber, *Integral Spirituality,* p. 159.

8. Bernadette Roberts, *The Path to No-Self* (Boston: Shambhala Publications, 1985), p. 141.

CHAPTER 2. THE WAY OF THE HEART

1. Kabir Helminski, *Living Presence: A Sufi Guide to Mindfulness and the Essential Self* (New York: Tarcher/ Putnam, 1992), p. 157.

2. Ibid., p. 158.

3. Sidney H. Griffith, "Merton, Massignon, and the Challenge of Islam," in Rob Barker and Gray Henry, eds., *Merton and Sufism: The Untold Story* (Louisville, KY: Fons Vitae, 1999), p. 65.

4. For extensive bibliographical information on this work, see "A Treatise on the Heart," translated by Nicholas Heer, in Ibid., pp. 79–88.

5. E. Kadloubovsky and E. M. Palmer, eds., *The Art of Prayer: An Orthodox Anthology* (London: Faber and Faber, 1966), p. 194.

6. Ibid., p. 190.

7. Robert Sardello, *Silence: The Mystery of Wholeness* (Benson, NC: Goldenstone Press, 2006), p. 82.

8. Ibid.

9. Ibid., p. 86.

10. No wonder the embodied aspect of heart spirituality is so important! For if Sardello is right here (and my own work confirms that he is), then the stunning conclusion is that *there is no lack.* That primordial hunger for intimacy and belonging we so frantically project onto others in our attempt to find fulfillment is *fulfilled already,* there in the "infinity of love" already residing holographically in our own hearts, once we have truly learned to attune to its frequency and trust that with which it reverberates. In this sense, our physical heart is the quintessential "treasure buried in the field."

11. Joseph Chilton Pearce, *The Biology of Transcendence* (Rochester, VT: Park Street Place, 2002).

12. Stephen Harrod Buhner, *The Secret Teachings of Plants: The Intelligence of the Heart in the Direct Perception of Nature* (Rochester, VT: Bear and Company, 2004).

13. Ibid., p. 71.

14. Pearce, pp. 64–65.

15. For a particularly clear and forceful discussion of this point, see E. Kadloubovsky and G. E. H. Palmer, trans., *Unseen Warfare* (New York: St. Vladimir's Seminary Press, 1987), pp. 241–44.

16. Reproduced in my *Centering Prayer and Inner Awakening* (Boston: Cowley Publications, 2004), p. 136.

17. Sardello, p. 72.

18. Rainer Maria Rilke, *Duino Elegies,* trans. J. B. Leischman and Stephen Spender (New York: Norton, 1939), p. 21.

19. Sardello, p. 72.

CHAPTER 3. CENTERING PRAYER AND ATTENTION OF THE HEART

1. Peter Feldmeier, "Centering Prayer and the Christian Contemplative Tradition," *Spiritual Life* (Winter 2003), p. 239.

2. Patrick Hart, ed., *Thomas Merton, Monk* (Garden City, NY: Image Books, 1976), p. 90.

3. For more on this point see my *Centering Prayer and Inner Awakening* (Cambridge, MA: Cowley Publications, 2004), chapter 5, "Spiritual Non-Possessiveness."

4. Shared in a private conversation with Robin Amis in September 1992 as we collaborated on his new edition of the collected writings of Theophan the Recluse. Robin Amis, ed., *Theophan the Recluse: Writings on Prayer of the Heart* (Newburyport, MA: Praxis Press, 1992).

5. Ira Progoff, ed., *The Cloud of Unknowing* (New York: Delta Books, 1957), p. 72.

6. John Cassian, *Conferences,* trans. Colm Luibheid (Mahwah, NJ: Paulist Press, 1985), p. 133. Cassian's full explanation runs as follows: "It carries within it a cry to God in the face of every danger. It expresses the humility of a pious confession. It conveys the watchfulness born of unending worry and fear. It conveys the sense of our frailty, the assurance of being heard, the confidence in help that is always and everywhere present."

7. Joseph Chu-Cong, *The Contemplative Experience*

(New York: Crossroad, 1999), p. 27. This goal, in fact, comprises the basic pedagogy of monastic love mysticism, which has flowed like a great underground river through the spirituality of the Christian West, reaching its culmination in the writings of Saint Bernard of Clairvaux. Father Chu-Cong's book is a profound yet accessible introduction to this great tradition.

8. E. Kadloubovsky and G. E. H. Palmer, trans., *Writings from the "Philokalia" on Prayer of the Heart* (London and Boston: Faber and Faber, 1951, 1992), pp. 152–61.

9. Ibid., p. 153.

10. Ibid.

11. Ibid.

12. Ibid., p. 154. In this context the word "heart" obviously refers to what we would today call "the unconscious," a nuance unavailable to Simeon.

13. Ibid., p. 158.

14. Jacob Needleman, *Lost Christianity* (New York: Doubleday, 1980), p. 162. The quotation from Simeon is from the *Philokalia,* p. 158.

15. This aspect of the sacred word has been consistently emphasized in the teachings of Father Basil Pennington. For further comments, see my preface to Thomas Keating and Basil Pennington, *Finding Grace at the Center* (Woodstock, VT: Skylight Paths, 2007).

16. Thomas Merton, *The Inner Experience: Notes on Contemplation,* William H. Shannon, ed. (San Francisco: HarperCollins, 2003), p. 44. The work was originally published as a series called "The Contemplative Experience" in several successive issues of *The Cistercian Review* in 1983. My original introduction to this quotation was through a photocopy of one of these articles loaned to me by a monk of Saint Benedict's Abbey, Snowmass, Colorado, in 1995.

CHAPTER 4. CENTERING PRAYER AS WITNESSING PRACTICE

1. Gerald May's take on the inner observer or witness was first laid out in his *Will and Spirit* (San Francisco: Harper and Row, 1982), a groundbreaking study in the intertwining paths of spirituality and psychology. See particularly pp. 95–100 and 214–16. His opinion is shared by his colleague Tilden Edwards, whose book, *Embracing the Call to Spiritual Depth: Gifts for Contemplative Living* (Mahwah, NJ: Paulist Press, 2010), continues to reinforce this basic distrust of witnessing practice, seeing it as the opponent of "direct awareness." According to Edwards: "The observer is the eye of our ego self-image" and "the first thing we encounter when we try to experience our self-image" (p. 34). For an alternative presentation of witnessing and as it has traditionally been understood in schools of inner work— including a helpful distinction between the egoic spectator and authentic witnessing presence—see John Welwood, *Toward a Psychology of Awakening* (Boston: Shambhala Publications, 2000), chapter 8.

2. Following well-known Eastern models, Wilber presents witnessing presence as the fourth of five levels of consciousness. In ascending order, these five levels are gross, subtle, causal, witness, nondual. For a succinct overview, see Wilber, p. 74.

3. These twenty-four videos, taped by Father Keating in 1986–87 and collectively known as *The Spiritual Journey,* continue to serve as the core curriculum for advancing practitioners of Centering Prayer. They are available for purchase from Contemplative Outreach (www.contemplativeoutreach.org), the international membership organization of the "Keating school" of Centering Prayer.

4. Eckhart Tolle, *The Power of Now: A Guide to Spiritual Enlightenment* (Vancouver, BC: Namaste Publishing, 1997), p. 152.

5. Robert Sardello, *Silence: The Mystery of Wholeness* (Benson, NC: Goldenstone Press, 2008), p. 52.

6. James A. Walsh, ed., *The Pursuit of Wisdom, and Other Works by the Author of "The Cloud of Unknowing"* (New York: Paulist Press, 1988), p. 229.

7. The Gurdjieff Work, a comprehensive system of inner awakening with deep roots in the ancient wisdom traditions of Central Asia and the Near East, was developed and brought to the West by the enigmatic Armenian spiritual teacher G. I. Gurdjieff (1866–1949). By its own preference remaining somewhat hidden, it laid the foundation for the "esoteric awakening" of our own times, offering both a cosmology and a practical methodology for awakening and inner transformation.

8. These reflections were shared between Tilden Edwards and myself in an e-mail exchange in September 2009.

9. Kadloubovsky and Palmer, *Philokalia*, p. 154.

10. Ibid.

11. In fact, this is the principal distinction between Centering Prayer and its sister method, the Christian meditation of John Main, where the insistence is that attention must be tethered on the mantra.

12. Jalal al-Din Rumi, "The Watermill," in *The Essential Rumi*, Coleman Barks, ed. (San Francisco: HarperCollins, 1995), pp. 247–48.

13. Beatrice Bruteau, "Prayer and Identity," in *Spirituality, Contemplation, and Transformation: Writings on Centering Prayer by Thomas Keating and Others* (New York: Lantern Books, 2008), p. 84.

14. Ibid., p. 101.

15. Ibid., p. 102.

16. Ibid.

17. Ibid., p. 99.

18. Kadloubovsky and Palmer, *Philokalia,* p. 153.

19. At the forefront of this work is the very interesting data being accumulated by the California-based HeartMath Institute. For an insightful overview of this research, see Pearce, p. 55–73.

20. While the practice is typically directed toward "afflictive emotions" (as they are known in the terminology of Centering Prayer), it works equally well—and with even more powerful effect—on the unbalanced pleasurable emotions generated by the *appeasement* of the false-self "programs for happiness." Here its pedigree as an authentic witnessing practice (not merely a therapeutic practice for the relief of symptoms) comes strongly to the fore.

21. Maurice Nicoll, *Psychological Commentaries on the Teachings of Ouspensky and Gurdjieff* (Boston and London: Shambhala Publications, 1984) vol 5, p. 1542.

CHAPTER 5. FURTHER TO SIMEON
THE NEW THEOLOGIAN

1. Needleman, pp. 155–62.

2. Kadloubovsky and Palmer, *Philokalia,* p. 158.

3. Ibid., p. 154.

4. This is the one shortcoming that detracts from the otherwise first-rate work of the HeartMath interpretation. The interpretation of the data and practices emerging from it are primarily visualization-based techniques to replace negativity with positivity. The alternative, equanimity, is not even considered.

5. Dylan Thomas, "This Side of the Truth," in *The Collected Poems of Dylan Thomas* (New York: New Directions, 1946) p. 117.

6. If this instruction somehow escapes notice in the original

texts themselves, I would call attention to the excellent reiteration of the point by Olga Louchakova, a contemporary initiate in this tradition, in her brilliant exploration of the Jesus Prayer in "The Essence of Prayer of the Heart," originally published as a chapter in Lee Lozowick's book of poetry, *Gasping for Air in a Vacuum* (Hohm Press, 2004, pp. 37–48) but more easily available online at www.researchgate.net. Many people assume that this prayer consists of the uninterrupted repetition of the name of Jesus, but this is not the full story: rather, it is the repetition of the name, while one's attention is "grounded in the sense of self in the chest" (p. 39). The following description deserves careful consideration:

> To start the practice search for the embodied sense of the self on the right side of the chest. This is the external expression of the subtle center of individuation. Ramana calls thus sense "aham-sphurana" (Sanskrit), the radiance of the I. St. Simeon the New Theologian, a 10th century Hesychast, calls it "the place where all the powers of the soul reside." To work with this center, one must have a developed capacity to keep one's attention "in," not "on." One has to keep the focus from slipping away into the lower centers of consciousness in the body, or from jumping up into the head. Concentration on locations other than this center will cause the practitioner to recycle through the lower domains of the ego, or to be stuck in discursive thought. The journey is through the Gnostic "mind of the heart," not the rationality of the head. One also has to have developed skills of mindfulness, with the capacity to differentiate the modalities of awareness, such as sensing, feeling, imagining, and thinking. The Christian analogue of mindfulness is called "wakefulness," "guarding the senses," "guarding the

heart," and it is characterized by the capacity to bounce back from the object of awareness onto the witnessing subjectivity (pp. 39–40).

CHAPTER 6. CENTERING PRAYER: PERSPECTIVES FROM THE NEUROSCIENCES

1. Since 1987 the Dalai Lama has hosted regular dialogues with leading scientists and neuroscientists, at his home in exile in Dharamsala. These "Mind and Life" dialogues laid the groundwork for the first formal conference of the Mind and Life Institute in Washington, DC, in 2007, continuing at regular intervals thereafter. In addition, His Holiness has had an active personal involvement in research programs in several North American universities, including Stanford and Emory.
2. This is the title of Sharon Begley's 2007 best seller, still one of the better nonspecialist introductions to the field. Sharon Begley *Train Your Mind, Change Your Brain* (New York: Ballantine Books, 2007).
3. Andrew Newberg and Mark Robert Waldman, *How God Changes Your Brain* (New York: Ballantine Books, 2009), p. 194.
4. Ibid.
5. Ibid., p. 194–95.
6. The notion that meditation methods have their distinctive neurological signature has been "out there" for some time now, but only very recently has the technology evolved to the point of being able to examine this hypothesis with real scientific rigor. In the early days of neuroscience there was an initial flurry of interest in matching meditation practices with brain-wave frequencies (delta, theta, alpha, beta), and some of this "information" still circulates in the popular literature. A second wave of interest came in the early years of this century with an increased capacity to

measure gamma-wave activity and patterns of brain-wave synchrony. In a pioneering 2004 study led by Antoine Lutz, a team of neuroscientists carefully monitored gamma-wave activity in a group of Tibetan Buddhist adepts; their findings are summarized in the title of the paper itself: "Long-Term Meditators Self-Induce High-Amplitude Gamma Synchrony during Mental Practice." (*Proceedings of the Natural Academy of Science* (PNAS) 101:46 [November 16, 2004], pp. 16369–16373). While this widely respected study is still a benchmark in its field, enthusiasm about gamma-wave synchrony has increasingly waned in light of the discovery that these waves are also attributable to extraneous muscle motions, such as eye blinks and external movements. A more sophisticated instrumentation now permits the analysis of waves into their individual components and sources of origin within the brain; this technology forms the basis for a new study by Brent Field and Michael Spezio that I will be discussing just ahead in the text.

7. In our phone interview on July 9, 2015, however, Brent Field made it clear that proficiency cannot be measured simply in terms of years of experience. A few of the more recent meditators were able to generate brain-wave patterns analogous to those of meditators far their senior in years, and vice versa.

8. Donald W. Mitchell and James A. Wiseman, eds., *The Gethsemani Encounter: A Dialogue on the Spiritual Life by Buddhist and Christian Monastics* (New York: Continuum, 1999), p. 182. Field and Spezio's research collaborator Andrew Dreitcer reports that in his many conversations with Buddhist teachers, they often describe feeling "pulled" into a deeper sense, and this involves a complete release of "cognitive control" and attentional efforts.

9. This comment was made during our interview at Scripps College on August 27, 2015.

10. In fact, in a personal conversation on November 2, 2015, the Buddhist translator and scholar Ken McLeod commented that that is exactly how the Tibetan Buddhist term *dran pa* was translated up until this century: as "recollection" rather than "mindfulness."

11. In an e-mail exchange between myself and Michael Spezio, February 6, 2016.

12. Andrew Dreitcer, Brent Field, and Michael Spezio, "Mindfulness as Heartfulness: Recovering Remembrance, *Imitatio,* and Love for Mindfulness in Interdisciplinary Contemplative Studies" (unpublished). Dreitcer is also a longtime participant in the Mind and Life Institute and an active collaborator, together with Thupten Jinpa (the Dalai Lama's personal translator), in The Center for Compassion and Altruism Research and Education at Stanford University. With permission of the authors I have included the abstract of this monograph below:

> Contemplative Studies is an interdisciplinary area seeking to understand embodied mindfulness in relation to human flourishing. Scientific approaches to mindfulness tend to frame it as a set of skills for cognitive and biomedical enhancement, emphasizing mental/emotional control or focus while minimizing the roots of mindfulness within narrative traditions of virtue. Yet there is growing recognition that theologically rich ethical formation is at the heart of Contemplative Studies, such that mindfulness concepts require consideration of moral anthropologies. We present an account of mindfulness centered in *imitatio* of divine love, drawing on Christian perspectives within the Abrahamic traditions, including consideration of moral purpose within practices calling

for affective openness, or heartfulness. We suggest that
these emphases provide new avenues for theological collaborations with cognitive science.

13. Dreitcer, Field, and Spezio, p. 12. The authors are basing
their observations here on discussions of mindfulness
emerging from two groundbreaking interspiritual contemplative dialogues: Thomas Keating's ongoing Snowmass
Conferences and the Buddhist/Christian dialogue at
Gethsemani Abbey in June 1996.

14. In Christianity, this would be the deepest meaning of
"putting on the mind of Christ" and the traditional practices of *imitatio Christi* that support it. See Dreitcer, Field,
and Spezio, pp. 32–46.

15. For a fuller description of the Snowmass Dialogues, see
Dreitcer, Field, and Spezio, pp. 5–9. See also Nathaniel
Miles-Yepez, ed., *The Common Heart: An Experience
of Interreligious Dialogue* (New York: Lantern Books,
2006). This book contains an extensive account of both
the history and the proceedings of this groundbreaking
interspiritual contemplative dialogue.

16. Like secular mindfulness training, HeartMath moves
a bit too quickly to divert the field of operation toward
personal wellness rather than transformation of consciousness.

CHAPTER 7. CENTERING INTO THE CLOUD

1. Progoff, p. 76.

2. From here on when citing passages from *The Cloud,* I
will adopt Progoff's numbering convention: "6-3" means
chapter 6, paragraph 3.

3. James A. Walsh ed., *The Pursuit of Wisdom and Other
Works by the Author of the Cloud of the Unknowing*
(Mahwah, NJ: Paulist Press, 1988).

4. Ibid., p. 229.
5. James A. Walsh, ed., *Julian of Norwich: Showings* (Mahwah, NJ: Paulist Press, 1978).
6. William Johnston, ed., *The Cloud of Unknowing and The Book of Privy Counsel* (New York: Doubleday, 2005).
7. Carmen Acevedo Butcher, trans., *The Cloud of Unknowing* (Boston: Shambhala Publications, 2009).

CHAPTER 8. OBJECTLESS AWARENESS

1. This is a standard explanatory formula within Contemplative Outreach teaching, featured in the short introductory brochure, and in all introductory workshops.
2. For an insightful discussion of this point, see John Welwood, *Toward a Psychology of Awakening* (Boston: Shambhala Publications, 2002) pp. 56–63.
3. Walsh, *Pursuit of Wisdom*, p. 221.

CHAPTER 9. NOTHING BUT GOD

1. Ira Progoff, ed., *The Cloud of Unknowing* (New York: Delta, 1957) p. 61.
2. Ibid.
3. Ibid.
4. Phyllis Hodgson, ed., *The Cloud of Unknowing and The Book of Privy Counsel* (London: Oxford University Press, 1944). This is the original Middle English version by the Early English Text Society based on a compilation of the seventeen manuscript texts.
5. I had a lively conversation on this point with the late Phyllis Tickle, who could not pinpoint the first appearance of the slogan "The devil will get you if you make your mind a blank," but suspected like myself that it was yet another creation of the religious awakenings of the early twentieth century, which also saw the birth of Pentecostalism and the widespread belief in the rapture.

We both agreed that it bears the imprint of an articulated psychological concept of the unconsciousness (which would be the case by the late nineteenth century) and that it differs substantially from the received teachings of Christian tradition, which state (following Jesus, and as we have seen in the Simeon the New Theologian teaching on the second method of attention and prayer) that it is from the *heart* that the passions and evil impulses arise.

6. Kadloubovsky and Palmer, *Philokalia*, p. 153.
7. Constance Fitzgerald, "From Impasse to Prophetic Hope," *Proceedings of the Catholic Theological Society of America* 64 (2009), p. 41.
8. For a brief overview of this thorny spiritual problem, see my *Centering Prayer and Inner Awakening* (Boston: Cowley Publications, 2004), pp. 74–77.
9. Progoff, p. 25.

CHAPTER 10. THE HEART OF THE CLOUD

1. William Johnston, ed., *The Cloud of Unknowing* (New York: Doubleday/Image, 1973, 2005), p. 45.
2. Rainer Marie Rilke, *Letter to a Young Poet,* translated by Stephen Mitchell (Boston, Shambhala, 1993), pp. 49–50.
3. Thomas Merton, *The Hidden Ground of Love,* William H. Shannon, ed. (New York: Farrar, Straus and Giroux, 1985), p. 64.

CHAPTER 11. JOUSTING WITH THOUGHTS

1. Butcher, pp. 23–24.
2. Ever one to seize upon popular modern metaphors, Keating for a time in the early 1990s became captivated by the image of Pac-Man, the celebrated video game omnivore, and suggested in an early edition of his core text *Open Mind, Open Heart* (Warwick, NY: Amity House 1986) that the sacred word was like a Pac-Man, gobbling

up all the other thoughts. He has since reconsidered, and I believe that this metaphor has disappeared from more recent editions of his work.

3. Johnston, *The Cloud of Unknowing* (New York: Doubleday/Image, 1973) p. 48.

CHAPTER 12. THE ART OF CONTEMPLATION

1. His warning here is repeated almost verbatim by Jacob Boehme two centuries later in his "Fourth Treatise on True Resignation." See Jacob Boehme, *The Way to Christ,* Peter Erb, ed. (New York: Paulist Press, 1978), p. 114.

2. The reference here is to Mary (of Mary and Martha fame) in the Gospel account recorded in Luke 19:38–42, where Mary sits at Jesus's feet in rapturous contemplation, and he pronounces that "Mary has chosen the better part, and it will not be taken from her."

3. This metaphor for the progressive and interwoven nature of spiritual progress is introduced and extensively developed by Ken Wilber in chapter 9 of *Integral Spirituality,* 179ff.

4. Ibid., overleaf to page 68.

CHAPTER 13. THE MYSTERY OF LOVE

1. For more on this, see my *The Meaning of Mary Magdalene* (Shambhala, 2010), pp. 22–23.

2. Progoff, *The Cloud of Unknowing,* p. 91. (In Progoff's edition this passage is labeled 12-3.)

3. Butcher, p. 57.

4. The Taizé community is an ecumenical monastic order located in southeast France that invites people of different faiths to worship together. They are well known for their contemplative hymns and chants in many languages. This particular Spanish chant paraphrases a poem by Teresa of Âvila.

CHAPTER 14. SORROW OF BEING

1. Merton, *Hidden Ground,* p. 64.

CODA: THE ELASTIC UNIVERSE

1. Butcher, pp. 13–14.

GOING FORWARD

1. Remember that favorite motto of a decade or so ago, "Contemplative Outreach is not an organization but an *organism!*"
2. The more intriguing possibility is that this addition of this new "heart-mode" of perception would be not a new line but a new *degree,* transforming the whole diagram into three dimensions.

INDEX